Practical
Communication

Francis J. Bergin

B.A., F.C.I.S., F.S.C.A., F.A.I.A., L.G.S.M., F.R.S.A.

Practical Communication

Second edition

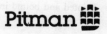

PITMAN PUBLISHING
128 Long Acre, London WC2E 9AN

A Division of Longman Group UK Limited

© F. J. Bergin 1976, 1981

First published in Great Britain 1976
Second edition 1981
Reprinted 1982, 1984, 1987, 1988, 1990

Printed and bound in Singapore

ISBN 0 273 01629 6

Contents

Preface

Because the communication of ideas and information in business and society is becoming more important each year Pitmans have decided to publish this second edition of *Practical Communication*. This edition is revised and considerably enlarged and it teaches you to communicate correctly from the start and, within its compass, it tells you what not to do as well as what you ought to do.

It is based on many years of practical experience in the teaching and practice of communications. Besides being designed as an operating manual for the business and professional man and woman, it also covers adequately the syllabi of the various professional bodies which now examine in Communications, particularly the Institute of Chartered Secretaries and Administrators, the Association of International Accountants and the Institute of Administrative Accounting. These bodies have kindly given permission for past examination questions to be included in this edition and where they appear they are identified by the initials ICSA, AIA and InstAA. This book is presented as an addition to the limited corpus of professional knowledge in the field of communications and in the belief that those who use it will benefit from both its practical and its academic standpoint.

It is particularly commended to students and examinees (including those for the new BEC courses) as being one of the few books published which caters specifically for their needs.

In areas where there has been a lacuna in my own knowledge I have called on the experience and learning of others. Mr. Barry Maude contributed the chapters on Communicating with Employees and In-company Communication Barriers, much of the material being drawn from his own book *Practical Communication for Managers* (Longman). Chapters fourteen to seventeen were very ably written by Mr. Peter Biddlecombe.

I should like to express my grateful thanks to the publishers for their helpful comments, constructive criticisms and encouragement throughout the book's preparation and to my secretary, Miss J. Q. Scott, for reading and correcting the manuscript.

Nevertheless, any errors or omissions which remain are my own responsibility. Any comments, criticisms or suggestions for inclusion in later editions will be gratefully received.   *F. J. Bergin*

1 Introduction

'with words we govern men'

Disraeli

There is little doubt that 'communication' is an 'in' word at the present time. It has almost become a cult. The word itself is derived from the Latin *communicare* meaning to share and from the French *communis*, meaning common. As a simple example of this meaning let us consider the American rattlesnake—not the most popular of creatures. If you ever come across one of these he will, in all probability, 'rattle' his tail. Why? To warn you that he is around and really does not want to bite you, so he hopes you will both hear and heed his warning rattle. You may have felt up to now that he was always being just plain objectionable. Not so. The problem is that we have never had much in common with rattlesnakes and there is therefore what we have come to call a 'communications barrier'. This illustrates that where we communicate with others we need to have something in common.

The necessity of communicating

Effective communication skills are required to deal successfully with all your associates and they are some of the most important skills you need if you want to raise yourself in management. Communication is the way management gets its job done and good managers are usually good communicators. Repeatedly, business disasters are attributed to failure in communications. Our need to communicate is universal and good communication is the hallmark of good morale. Analyse the job of any successful manager you know, and you will find that he is primarily a communicator.

The *Concise Oxford Dictionary* defines the word 'communicate' as to impart, transmit or share. It is true to say therefore that effective communication depends more on the sender's attitude towards the receiver than on the sender's gifts for writing or for speaking in front of an audience. Communication is far less a technique than an attitude, and it is unfortunate that much of our attitude towards the subject has been developed from the recognition of the negative effect of bad communication rather than the positive effect of good communication.

1

Most of a business manager's time is spent in:

(1)   passing information and ideas upwards to senior management to aid their decision-making;

(2)   providing other department managers with information which will help them do their jobs more effectively, i.e. lateral communication;

(3)   passing information downwards;

(4)   conveying attitudes or creating them;

(5)   receiving and interpreting facts from those working for him;

(6)   communicating with people outside his own company including customers, Government Departments, trade and professional institutes and the members of the general public.

The activities of any business and the series of relationships existing are kept in dynamic form by communication. Communications activate decisions, but clearly decisions without communications are useless, or with poor communications, ineffective. Much depends on the manager's power to inform and to persuade. Most businessmen today receive a good basic training in their specialized field but few, if any, have any formal training in communications. You may tend to be surprised occasionally throughout the remainder of this book by the simplicity of certain points which are discussed. Take for example the point you will come across about the timing of any presentation (chapter 2). You may think this very elementary—and it is! But ask yourself how often you have sat through a presentation that seemed to go on forever or think of the many times you endured a meeting which ended only through sheer exhaustion and was presided over perhaps by the chairman of the bored! Then just try to think of the talks you attended when you genuinely wished the speaker to go on for another half an hour. You can probably count these on the fingers of one hand.

In communication thoughts and ideas are transferred from one mind to another either by speech or the recorded written word. Both the speaking and the writing may be assisted or replaced by pictorial matter but all basic communicating involves the use of words. One of the riches of the English language is the variety of words which may be put together so as to say the same thing in many different ways. But again, particularly in written communications, words have meanings which are not always identical for different people. So we must attempt to be precise, otherwise our message may be misunderstood by others (or, if you like, understood in a sense completely different from what we intended). To put it in the words of an old French proverb 'anything which can be misunderstood will be misunderstood'. So chapter 12 deals with precision in the writing of instructions, letters and reports.

2 The Communication Process

'Think like a wise man but communicate in the language of the people'

W. B. Yeats

There is little doubt that, because of the lack of a proper understanding of the principles and processes of communication, many a good idea has never travelled beyond the mind of its creator. When we talk of communicating we talk of the transmission of information in its widest sense. We consider messages, facts, ideas and opinions as well as feelings and emotions, some of which we indicate to others without ever realizing we are doing so. Almost every communicator generates an intermingled pattern of fact and feeling. Because of this you may find yourself in an intricate web of human relations woven of emotions and sentiments as well as thoughts and ideas. Words happen to be our main tools in communicating, though they are fragile verbal tools often dulled by wrong usage and for many of us not always readily to hand! Nevertheless they are the only medium through which we may make ourselves understood by others. We are all a complex mixture of thoughts, feelings, ideas and emotions. For example, we cherish privacy but thrive on friendship. We are individual and we are unique. Yet we must live and work with others, and in doing so make daily use of the process of communication. Graphically the communications process looks something like Fig. 1.

You will see from this that there are many areas where misunderstandings can easily creep in. Our task therefore does not end when the message is dispatched. We must make sure it has been received, and, more importantly, that it has been considered and understood. Barriers of all kinds abound in this communication process, and people will tell you 'it's not what you say but how you say it'. There is some truth in this but it is by no means the whole truth.

The grapevine
Witness for a moment the office 'grapevine' which combines fact, inference and judgment. It is an amateur system. It is unplanned, uncoordinated and employs largely fortuitous channels of information flow.

4

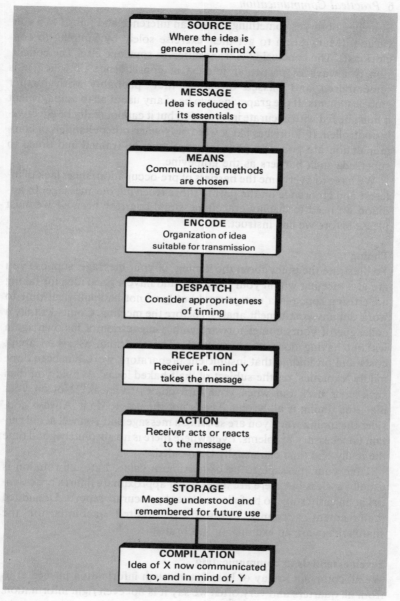

```
        ┌─────────────────────────┐
        │         SOURCE          │
        │   Where the idea is     │
        │  generated in mind X    │
        └─────────────────────────┘

        ┌─────────────────────────┐
        │         MESSAGE         │
        │   Idea is reduced to    │
        │      its essentials     │
        └─────────────────────────┘

        ┌─────────────────────────┐
        │          MEANS          │
        │  Communicating methods  │
        │       are chosen        │
        └─────────────────────────┘

        ┌─────────────────────────┐
        │         ENCODE          │
        │   Organization of idea  │
        │  suitable for transmission │
        └─────────────────────────┘

        ┌─────────────────────────┐
        │        DESPATCH         │
        │ Consider appropriateness │
        │        of timing        │
        └─────────────────────────┘

        ┌─────────────────────────┐
        │        RECEPTION        │
        │   Receiver i.e. mind Y  │
        │     takes the message   │
        └─────────────────────────┘

        ┌─────────────────────────┐
        │         ACTION          │
        │   Receiver acts or reacts │
        │     to the message      │
        └─────────────────────────┘

        ┌─────────────────────────┐
        │         STORAGE         │
        │  Message understood and │
        │ remembered for future use │
        └─────────────────────────┘

        ┌─────────────────────────┐
        │       COMPILATION       │
        │ Idea of X now communicated │
        │  to, and in mind of, Y  │
        └─────────────────────────┘
```

Fig. 1

Someone observes something, makes an inference and jumps to a conclusion. (Many seem to get their exercise solely by jumping to conclusions!). The conclusion is transmitted to someone else. The conclusion is always of particular interest in consequence of which it is remembered and passed on as a 'fact' probably with further embellishments. If the grapevine is to be of any use at all to management it must be fed with accurate information but it cannot really be effectively controlled. It flourishes like a weed only when other channels of communication are poor. So your message must be framed and timed to supersede such barriers as the grapevine.

We have to overcome the barriers of pre-occupation, sheer lack of interest and ignorance on the part of those receiving our message. In addition we need to display gracefulness and courtesy because we must please before we can instruct.

Timing
To illustrate the point about the 'timing' of your message, suppose you are at a meeting within your company and have a good idea for taking advertising space in a new journal but have not had sufficient time to work out any cost-benefit analysis before the meeting. Coincidentally a colleague of yours comes forward with a suggestion of his own again without having done much research. The chairman asks him about costs and on finding that insufficient preparatory work has been done mildly 'explodes' on the subject of 'half-baked ideas'. Would you then stick your neck out when your turn comes to speak? Not on your life—the timing is all wrong. That's not the day to do it. Always consider the timing when you are sending a message and you will avoid certain unnecessary problems. Even where there is no absolutely good time the really bad time can usually be avoided.

Time your message to be of maximum value. Late information is usually useless but there are times when approximate figures are essential at an early stage to be followed later by accurate reports. Unaudited management accounts followed by audited accounts for the shareholders are an example of this principle.

Seven essentials in communicating
We all complain to-day of having too much information pushed at us from all quarters and very often we say it is not even right information. Your message will therefore have competition, and in order for it to be considered it must be as concise as possible. But conciseness should

never be obtained at the cost of clarity, accuracy or appropriateness. Study the level of knowledge your reader or listener has reached and avoid using technical terms or jargon unless you are sure he or she will be able to understand them easily. One of the most important points to remember in communicating is to have your message express something and not impress someone. But your message should be as compelling and attractive as possible.

We can sum up by saying that there are seven 'c's' to remember in written or spoken communication. You need to be:

Candid
Clear
Complete
Concise
Concrete
Correct
Courteous.

Listening

So far we have not touched on a very significant area of communication—listening. Communication is a two-way process and listening is extremely important. Communicating does not merely mean talking or writing to people. It means transmitting a message to evoke a discriminating response. Listening is as much a part of communicating as is talking. Most of us have a certain built-in resistance when it comes to listening to others. This is a double-edged sword and most people are reluctant to listen to us too: one effective way of dismantling that barrier is by listening ourselves. If you don't listen you will become as emotion blind when you are dealing with people as some are colour blind.

One of the most successful businessmen in the Western world wrote these words towards the end of a long life:

'Most of us think we are pretty good listeners. I know when I started out in life I thought I was a good listener. But the longer I live the more I realize that listening is not something that comes naturally; it is an acquired art. For most of us, listening, whether in a social conversation or around the table at a conference, is just a pause we feel obliged to grant a speaker until we again have a chance to air our own opinions. This is not real listening in any sense of the word. Listening is not a passive activity during which we let our own thoughts intrude upon what someone else is saying. To actively listen to another person requires willpower, concentration and great mental effort. Its rewards are great, because only then do we really learn something about the other person—his feelings, his ambitions, his hopes, his aspirations, what kind of person he really is, what his complaints are and what he needs.

You'll be surprised how much more you can learn from others by listening in this way once you set your mind to it and how much it can help you in your work—whether with subordinates or superiors. There will be far fewer misunderstandings, senseless arguments and emotional outbursts. You will be much better equipped to appraise and evaluate the drives and needs of other people—subordinates, superiors, associates—from their point of view rather than your own'

(from *What Every Executive Should Know About Himself*, by J. C. Penney)

We must really listen and not just pretend to do so. We need the ability to become knowledgeable about what others think and feel. Without our listening that 'feel' will never be acquired. We listen to understand the attitudes of others. This involves us in hearing a lot more than words and involves us in the following up lines of approach suggested by the emotional overtones in what people say.

Points for discussion

'The formal communication network is often inadequate or too slow. In such cases the informal communication networks—often called the "grapevine"—spring into action to meet the needs of people'. Discuss. (AIA)

Define message competition.

What are the seven 'c's' of good communication?

Why is it generally felt that concise writing is important in business communications? (InstAA)

Effective listening is as important as effective speaking. Comment on this statement. (AIA)

3 Lines of Communication

'It is a luxury to be understood'

Emerson

When we talk of lines of communication we mean the channels through which information is transferred within an organization from one person to another. Communication, as we have already seen, is essentially a two-way process and information has not only to be sent but has also to be received and understood. It must be acted upon too. Machinery needs to be available through which there can be downward communication (from superior to subordinate), upward communication (from subordinate to superior) and horizontal communication which occurs between individuals of comparable status.

Careful attention must be paid to these lines of communication because internal communication is vital for the success of any business and it is a much more difficult process now than it was a few decades ago. The principal reason for this is that there has been a change in the attitude of workers to their employers and in the present industrial climate there has been a move away from the old concept that management could tell staff and workers what to do and expect unquestioning obedience. Proper provision must therefore be made for upward communication otherwise senior management, besides generating bad feeling, may end up making decisions in a vacuum and such decisions may not be readily accepted by the shop floor.   The basic questions which all of us who work have can be divided into two categories: (a) what, where, when, why, and how does my employer expect me to perform and (b) what, where, when, why and how will my work benefit my employer and me?

We will deal here mainly with a few technical aspects of lines of communication as the matter of barriers and attitudes is more fully covered in chapter 11.

Line management or vertical communication
By line organization we mean a vertical line organization where one rank is clearly seen below another to which it is directly related (Fig. 2).

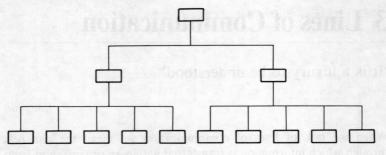

Fig. 2. Line organization

This simple chart shows clearly the need for two-way channels not only throughout any business organization but also indeed within each individual department because in almost every case there has to be this hierarchial structure in order to achieve the overall objectives of the business.

In setting up, or in reviewing, channels of communication it is absolutely necessary to draw up an organization chart which clearly spells out lines of authority and responsibility. Without knowing who does what and to whom he or she is responsible how on earth can you set up lines of communication? The task of preparing this organization chart also enables every unit to be brought under review and the relationships of the units one to another to be assessed. As a prelude to this exercise every single employee should have a detailed job description showing the job summary, the job content, and the job requirements in terms of skill and qualifications, besides mental and physical requirements.

When preparing an organization chart we must ensure that no employee is accountable to more than one superior and that the superior has full responsibility for those under his control. The larger the organization becomes, the more difficult it is for middle management to communicate because they have to receive instructions on the one hand and then interpret them and pass them down the line on the other. Perhaps of all groups it is these men and women who need to become expert in this field.

In parallel with these channels of communication in the line management function will be another communication line provided by the existence of a staff association or branches of trade unions. The representatives from these usually constitute the only intermediate stage between senior management and the rank and file. Part of a firm's total communication will pass up and down this line also and deciding what communication is more appropriate to the authority line and what to that of the staff representatives is a major problem for management. Indeed sometimes information should be passed down both lines. But there must be facility for two-way communication within line management otherwise frustrations are built up and all too soon attitudes begin to harden. It has been proven beyond a shadow of a doubt that the mere existence of upward communication channels can and does boost morale. This means that employees must be able to *initiate* communication as well as merely supplying feedback and it also means that these employee communications must be dealt with promptly otherwise the channels will come to be regarded as either a charade or an excuse for inactivity.

Difficulties in vertical communication

One problem about which little can be done is that of geographical location. But we should ensure that delays are as short as possible and that communication between branches and divisions is consistent and looks the same. Some companies manage to have such different systems of communication and varying stationery within their many divisions that the piece of written communication going from one to another looks as though it came from a competing company in Timbuktu.

There is also considerable difficulty when the line of communication or chain of command becomes too long. At each level through which communication flows there is a risk of some distortion so that at the end the message is liable to come out as though it had come through the party game of 'Chinese Whispers'! This is the case in the use of verbal instructions or information in particular.

Managers themselves must not be overburdened and their span of control should be sufficiently limited to ensure that they have to deal directly with no more than half a dozen subordinates for whose activities they are responsible.

Overcoming the difficulties

Frequent face-to-face contact with employees enables you to learn about their goals, abilities and ideals. It is vitally important in line management that manager and operative understand each other's point of view. There should be regular meetings where people are actively encouraged to discuss their grievances and job problems and if these are legitimate problems action must be taken immediately to solve them. Constructive criticisms should be welcomed however unpalatable they may appear at the time. Have an 'open door' policy if you are a manager and make sure that whoever comes through the door feels welcome and not inhibited or terrified in making their feelings known.

Upward communication is to be encouraged and above all must be *listened to*. Neither superior nor subordinate should over rely on the formal communication machinery, works councils, committees, etc., but ensure that informal chats and exchanges take place regularly.

Horizontal communication

As mentioned earlier horizontal communication means communication between those of comparable status as is the case between one department head and another. In horizontal communication letters, memoranda and reports feature widely, all of which tend (if used correctly) to ensure that there is unimpeded communication between departments. One must be careful though to see that a feeling of competition does not develop between different departments as this only generates bad feeling and suspicion and indeed can eventually lead to whole areas of a business becoming watertight thereby completely blocking out horizontal communication altogether!

Effective horizontal communication depends a very great deal on the attitudes prevailing across departments and particularly between the heads of the various departments. One must watch out for any signs of demarcation lines becoming unnecessarily important as this always limits free communication as does any tendency towards 'empire building'.

Face-to-face communication is probably the best method of ensuring successful horizontal communication and is preferable to overuse of—enemy number one—the internal telephone which often gives rise to the usual distortions! Committee meetings are also very useful in horizontal communication provided they are properly chaired and don't go on for ever.

It is imperative that there exists good communication between specialist and line supervision too because it is in this area that misunderstandings are very likely to occur with disastrous results. Jargon should be used as little as possible between departments because, quite apart from often being misunderstood, it does create unnecessary barriers between different departments.

Points for discussion

What are the main channels of communication that can be used in a large organization to give information to employees? (ICSA)

In communicating there are certain advantages in what are known as 'face-to-face' exchanges. Enumerate those known to you. (InstAA)

What do we mean when we speak of a Manager's span of control?

'Enlightened managements consider it is just as important to keep employees informed as it is to keep shareholders informed'. Discuss the matters of interest to employees and suggest appropriate means of conveying the required information. (AIA)

Why do you consider it important for any business to have a clearly defined organization chart?

4 The Oral Presentation

'Blessed are they who have nothing to say and cannot be persuaded to say it'

Speaking in public, whether you define the public as ten people or ten thousand, is not the unusual event it used to be for the average man or woman. Even if you are not often asked to make a formal presentation you can hardly expect these days to avoid being called upon to speak from the floor on occasion. A speech implies three things: (a) a speaker; (b) a subject; and (c) an audience. The speech is really the connection between the three. However, I must point out that 'a subject' means *your* subject—one which you have thought about and on which you have some depth of feeling. Without this total commitment to the subject matter itself you will never persuade or move a group of people. And in a democratic society such as ours, and in a world that increasingly seeks to talk out its differences rather than fight them out, the ability to express ideas is just as essential as the capacity to have them in the first place.

Nervousness
Immediately we begin considering this subject of speaking in public you will say that one of the greatest barriers is nervousness. Well, if it's any help to you, I have given hundreds of presentations, seminars and lectures and I have never yet approached a lectern without feeling nervous. Over the years, that nervousness has obviously decreased, due principally to practice coupled with a healthy refusal to speak dogmatically (or indeed at all) on matters of which I know little. And I have come to treat with scepticism the statement 'Oh, I'm never really nervous when giving a talk'. It is generally true that a degree of nervousness helps your presentation and gives you what physiologists call 'muscle tonus'. A person who is never slightly nervous usually does a mediocre job. Doubtless there are a few gifted individuals who have no need to feel uneasy but they are very rare indeed.

Mark Twain said that the first time he stood up to lecture he felt as if his mouth were filled with cotton wool and his pulse were speeding for some prize cup. Disraeli admitted that he would rather have led a cavalry charge than have faced the House of Commons for the first

14

time, and at the end he was its favourite speaker. I have personally known of a speaker to collapse physically twice while trying to propose a toast during a professional institute's annual dinner, and I have seen people literally dry up and fail to utter a single word when faced with the ordeal (real or imagined) of making a speech. Cicero said two thousand years ago that all public speaking of real merit was characterized by nervousness.

I do realize that all of this may not, when you come to speak, prove of much encouragement to you! So let's take a look at the positive side of things.

Remedies for nervousness

The greatest aid in the fight against 'nerves' is preparation. There is no substitute for adequate thorough preparation. Knowing more about your subject than your audience must be an effective weapon in your armour. A talk grows. From an idea you will gradually gather supporting material and statistics, remember relevant experiences unique to you as a person and you will take the opportunity of discussing your intended line of approach with colleagues beforehand. We will consider preparation fully in a later chapter, but suffice it to say now that while good preparation and good presentation are both vital in any talk you give, the extent and quality of preparation are infinitely more important, significant and essential than the manner of presentation. A good speaking (or writing) ability is no substitute for adequate knowledge of your subject.

Remember that an audience expects you to be slightly nervous, but you have an advantage over them in that they do not know exactly how nervous you really are! Audiences, too, tend inwardly to wish you success as it is as much of an embarrassment to them as it is to you if you botch up your assignment. One mistake I've seen several speakers make is to assume that their audience will be hostile. This is fatal. Although some may be in that frame of mind the majority certainly won't. But it will greatly help if you glance particularly (without staring) at someone you know well and whom you believe to be particularly sympathetic. Even if you do not know a member of the audience personally there are always at least two or three who look friendlier than the others, so concentrate on those who look more receptive and this will encourage you.

The sound of our own voices and being the centre of attraction do pose slight problems for us all. Therefore you will need to practice as much as possible. You can always take the opportunity of commenting briefly at meetings you attend as a delegate or of asking a question during a public meeting, gradually to get used to hearing yourself speak in public. Occasional use of a tape recorder is excellent, as this gives a fairly accurate reproduction of your own voice.

When called upon to speak do not let nervousness make you start speaking as you rise from your chair, or your audience will wonder what you are mumbling about as you rise to address them. Just come to the rostrum and look your audience in the eye for just a few seconds—then firmly say 'Good afternoon, Ladies and Gentlemen' (provided it is not morning!) and you are away to a good start with the full attention of your audience.

The four methods of delivery

Before we look at the essential elements in any oral presentation it is well for us to look at the four most commonly used methods of preparing and delivering a speech.

Writing out the presentation and reading it

This method of preparing and delivering a talk is probably the worst. It is bad because we do not speak as we write. Writing gives us time for careful selection of words, for working out sentences that are long and involved, and for what we call in general terms 'polish'. All of this deprives the speech of its directness and validity. When your speech is written you will go over it carefully and, noticing some 'common' word, you will probably think that a better word can be substituted, by which you mean a bigger word. You will tend to do this several times. You will also notice a number of short sentences, and you will combine them into one long sentence. Thus while the audience are trying to determine the sense of your last sentence you will be half way through the next one. This will go on until the written speech is far removed in style and manner from that of direct conversation, whereas the conversational approach is absolutely necessary in putting any point across to a group of people. As a result of your changes in style the audience notices the difference, finds greater difficulty in understanding your points and, fatigued by the difficulty, grows restless and inattentive, and maybe even 'dozes off'. The speech loses the effect of sincerity. The audience feels you are telling them not what you think and feel about the subject at the moment but what you thought about it a week or ten days before, and so much of its power is lost. Any speech must be phrased as to seem original and interesting throughout, and to be stamped with the personality of the speaker. In addition to the disadvantage already mentioned the power of the eye is lost, and your eye is one of the most important agents of expression. Your eyes make the first electrical connection with your audience; they turn on the current. By the eyes many of the most subtle and telling effects are secured by a speaker. The voice will also follow an entirely different pattern from that of normal conversation. The vocal apparatus is usually cramped and misdirected in reading. Nearly always the person who reads his speech directs his voice towards the manuscript, the lectern or the floor rather than out towards the audience, and it is almost impossible to avoid a monotonous pitch.

Some advantages in reading an address. But in spite of these disadvantages there definitely are occasions when the reading of a carefully prepared address seems fitting. Government Ministers often write out and read their speeches to avoid being misquoted. Generally the occasions on which such men speak are important and great care must be exercised in determining what is said. At certain other times of a somewhat formal or ceremonial character such as a Speech Day or the anniversary of the founding of some institution, a carefully prepared speech read from typescript may seem in order. On such occasions the speaker is often invited long beforehand, and is supposed to have devoted much time and thought to what he has to say. A typescript lives up to this presumption and seems to add worth and dignity. Further, these addresses are often printed afterwards, and it is well to have them in such exact and definite form as will bring out their literary merit. Because careful statement is needed, and as figures and statistics often occur, technical addresses may well be read from typescript.

Writing out a speech and committing it to memory

This method has many of the same faults that are found in the method of writing out and reading your talk. The language used is stilted and artificial, and the sentence structure is often involved with the effects carefully studied. Again, no chance is given in a committed speech for adaption to unforeseen circumstances either in the occasion or the audience. The talk must be delivered as it was committed to memory, for if any changes are made, or if heckling breaks out, the association of ideas by which the various sentences are remembered is destroyed, and it is well-nigh impossible to pick up the thread of the speech again. Further, your whole personality cannot react to the audience at the time of speaking. Your mind will be busily engaged in remembering words and sentence forms and cannot devote adequate attention to re-creating the thought while speaking. Any gestures are likely to be ill-timed, to be just a fraction of a second too early or too late. When gestures are developed for their own sakes and when they are practised as something apart from the thought, they are unlikely to be very successful in revealing your true feelings of the moment (if indeed there be any real feeling in a committed speech).

Another objection that applies to writing and committing a speech to memory is that it involves a tremendous amount of time and effort. It is no small task just pushing a pen through the words of a thirty-minute speech, and when the additional work of committing these words to memory is imposed, the task becomes staggering.

But the greatest objection to this method is that the whole thing is likely to be forgotten. The memory is one of the most unreliable functions of the mind, and scarcely is there a speaker who uses the memoriter style who has not gone through the excruciating experience of forgetting.

The extemporaneous method

The third method of preparing and delivering a talk is known as the extempore or extemporaneous method. By this we mean that the outline or path of thought is carefully prepared, so that the speaker knows beforehand just what thoughts he or she will utter but leaves the exact language in which these thoughts will be clothed until appearance before the audience. This method takes a middle course, and is the one usually employed by most good speakers. This extempore style should be carefully distinguished from the impromptu style, by which is meant that the speaker prepares neither thought nor words before the actual speaking. It must be said in regard to the impromptu style that very little good speaking generally results from it. Impromptu speeches are likely to be loosely built and of slight material. They are, in the words of the late Lord Goddard, 'usually not worth the paper they are written on'.

However, you will no doubt be called upon from time to time for an impromptu speech or at least a few intelligent words, so we will look at some formulae later on which will help you when that critical hour does arrive.

In the extemporaneous method the thoughts are never left to the moment. The speaker knows his goal exactly and the means he will employ to reach it.

Notes. Whether notes should be carried before the audience or not depends entirely on your own feelings and on the complexity of your outline. If you find it easy to carry an outline in your mind you should by all means do this and not depend on notes. On the other hand if you have some difficulty in remembering an outline there is nothing wrong in carrying notes on the platform. But let me say that no attempt should be made to conceal them. They should not be hidden in the palm of your hand or behind your back (or, as I have seen several times, partially pushed up a jacket sleeve!). The notes should be typed on one side only of cards about the size of a postcard or smaller (3 in × 5 in are ideal) and the writing or typing should be large enough to allow you to catch the words from the waistline, so that there will be no need to lift the card close to your eyes in order to catch the next headline. Never write your notes on both sides of a card—it will always be the wrong side up when you need the notes!

The card(s) should not be folded, for often the card is found to be folded just when the notes are needed and a pause in the presentation is necessary while you unfold the card and find the desired place. Neither should the cards be rolled up. Generally speaking, notes should not be written on large sheets of paper, for the tendency is to fold the paper while speaking and once again the notes are not ready for instant use when needed. And sheets of paper tend to distract your listeners.

Headings. The catch words of which the notes are made up should always contain some idea or topic. Avoid notes that merely give you the first words of a sentence or paragraph but do not contain an idea. Such phrases as 'it was once said' or 'another thing is' are useless because you cannot remember the idea which they were meant to suggest. If the topic is Gas Cookers, for example, the heads could be 'Economy of Gas', 'Ease of Manipulation', 'After Sales Service', etc. The notes should never be laid on the desk in front of you because you will nearly always find yourself some distance away from the desk when you need to refer to them, and you may also have to keep bending over to see them, thus taking your eyes off your audience. If you lay your notes on the desk and then walk out in front of it you will find you have to step back quickly, creating an awkward pause while you frantically find your place. (I am always doing this myself, and never seem to learn the lesson.)

Notes, then, should be written on cards, clearly numbered, one side only being used, in writing large enough to be seen from the waist-line and should be used without any effort at concealment.

People raise numerous objections to the extempore speech. It is said

that slang and colloquial expressions abound in it, that there is unnecessary repetition and diffuseness, and that the sentence structure is
faulty. Grammar is often poor, and the speaker sometimes makes rash
and ill-considered statements. All these charges are, doubtless, at one
time or another justified, but these faults are in the practice of the
method and not the method itself. Persistent practice and supplemen-
tary study should be engaged in until these faults are eliminated. It does
take a longer time to perfect the extemporaneous style of speaking but,
all things considered, the freedom and excellence it finally gives you fully justify its being called the best style.

The combination style

Sometimes speakers use a combination of styles. One may write and
read in part and speak from memory in part. Or you may write and read
in some portions and extemporize in others. Or you may extemporize
on the whole but introduce portions delivered from memory.

Whatever combinations of style a speaker uses it will probably be
found that the result is 'spotty'. The audience is normally well aware
that there has been a change in style, and attention will be taken from
the speech and expended upon watching the speaker and his varying
methods, or the audience will pay attention to the parts it likes—which
are usually the extemporized parts—and will not listen so attentively to
the other parts.

It is absolutely essential to give careful attention to the wording of the
opening (and closing) of your talks, and some practice may be pursued
in regard to these few sentences. Further than this you should trust to
the moment for your exact language. Remember: talk *to* your audience
and not *at* them.

Now let's take a look at the essentials of any oral presentation.

Points for discussion

What do you consider the best antidote to 'nerves'?

What are the four principal methods of delivering an oral presentation and which do you recommend speakers to use? Give reasons.
(InstAA)

Should notes be used while making a speech?

Impromptu speeches show sincerity of purpose. Comment.

Why should speeches not be read before an audience as a general
rule?

What, in your view, are the main advantages of the spoken word over all other forms of business communication? (InstAA)

'The best system of communication is that achieved with the least paperwork'. Say how far you agree with this statement and explain the advantages of (a) oral, (b) written communication in business (ICSA).

5 Preparation, Introduction and Conclusion

'The ability to speak effectively is an acquirement rather than a gift'

William Jennings Bryan

Remote preparation

There are few formal occasions when you will have a speaking engagement thrust upon you with only a few days' notice. Normally, even for business presentations and lectures, there will be a week or two for thought and preparation. From the moment you agree to your assignment until a day or two beforehand you can and should engage in what is called 'Remote Preparation', which consists of five essential steps.

(1) Determining the presentation's purpose.
(2) Analysing the occasion and the audience.
(3) Selecting and narrowing the subject matter.
(4) Gathering and selecting the material.
(5) Outlining your presentation.

Determining the presentation's purpose

It is insufficient to centre your speech around a certain subject—you really must ask: What response do I want from my audience? Do I want to amuse or entertain them? Do I want them to buy my product or service? Do I want their support for a cause, or do I want them to understand a difficult academic point? You must think of your speech as an instrument to be used in getting a definite reaction. Write your purpose out in a single sentence, so that it becomes the criterion by which you judge whether or not to include any of the subsequent points that come into your mind. This is the foundation stone in building any talk—your specific purpose statement (SPS). Be ruthless in this exercise—anything which does not add to or support this purpose is out.

Analysing the occasion and the audience

Think clearly of the occasion. How formal will it be? How many are expected to attend? Most of us have found that some speeches at wed-

22

dings, coming-of-age parties, etc., are hardly ever worth listening to. This is because they are always thought to be easy and are put together on the back of an envelope or cigarette packet at the last minute. No serious preparation or judicious balance of the witty and serious remark means a sloppy speech. Consider carefully what the occasion will demand. Every talk, however witty, should have a connecting thread running throughout.

Consider your audience very carefully. What brings them together? What will their probable attitude be to you and your subject? Will they be professional people, businessmen, or civil servants? Will they be young or old? If they are young then don't keep talking about the First or Second World Wars. Young people must be treated with courtesy and without any trace of condescension. Will your listeners be well versed in your topic or not? One rule to remember is this: never overestimate their intelligence nor underestimate their knowledge. If you are in serious doubt about these matters it is worth having a session with someone who will be in the audience or someone who comes from the same professional group as those attending; this will help you discover the level of interest, information, experience, understanding, prejudice and resistance that you should expect to find in your audience. Do not plan to ask your audience for any response that you cannot reasonably expect from people with their attitudes and beliefs.

Always remember you are speaking to *express* and not to impress!

Selecting and narrowing the subject matter
Sometimes your subject will be chosen for you. Occasionally I get an invitation to speak 'about anything to do with such-and-so'. I always politely decline. I have accepted such assignments in the past, spoken (brilliantly of course!) throughout on a subject of my own choosing to the general surprise of the audience! They had no idea I was going to speak on that aspect of the subject. Beware. Agree the subject (if possible in detail) with the chairman of the meeting as soon as you agree to speak. It is too important a matter to leave to chance. At the same time ensure that the notice convening the meeting reflects your subject precisely. If you are expected to choose your own subject do make sure you opt for one on which you feel deeply, are vitally interested in, know thoroughly, and on which you can make a genuine contribution.

Dr Edward Everett Hale said: 'Before a speaker faces his audience, he should write a letter to a friend and say: 'I am to make an address on a subject, and I want to make these points'. He should then enumerate the things he is going to speak about in their correct order. If he finds that he has nothing to say in his letter, he had better write to the committee that invited him and say that the probable death of his grandmother will possibly prevent his being present on the occasion'.

Gathering and selecting the material

Having a clear goal for your presentation the next obvious step is to gather the material you will use. The SPS will greatly help you in selecting the material; anything not relevant thereto must be ruthlessly rejected. Don't end up like the author who, when challenged as to why he had written such a long book, said 'I did not have time to write a shorter one'.

From the very moment you agree to your assignment you must begin gathering the material. This includes selecting articles and quotations from newspapers, magazines, books and reports. Your secretary can be a great help in this particular task. You need facts, illustrations, instances, examples, and anecdotes. Causes and effects and statistics will be needed. Even a few jokes will be necessary. But be sure your facts are indeed facts and not mere assumptions or unproved assertions. Take nothing for granted.

Then you have the fairly simple task of bringing together what you already know of the subject, sifting it and making it ready for the detailed building of your presentation. It can be of help to sort out the various possible points into A, B and C columns: A for what must be included, B for what ought to be included, and C for what it would be worth saying if you had the time. Don't forget that while you will normally have ample time for this aspect of preparation your audience will not, and your facts and conclusions must be presented to them as a kind of pre-digested mental food which their minds can readily absorb. The facts and information must first pass through your mind as though it were a kind of filter. Be sure you use the familiar word in place of the unfamiliar, the concrete word in place of the abstract, the short word in place of the long and the single word in place of the circumlocution. Fancy language won't cover up or excuse fuzzy ideas—it results only in additional vagueness.

The good communicator is the person who can make himself clear to himself first. Most people are not clear because they do not really know what they are trying to say. Good style is not much more than good clean clear thinking. And the man who retains that stubbornness which says 'I don't understand that' learns how to make it clear to himself and then make it clear to others.

You will need to give your talk a title—the subject denotes the content of your speech: the problem to be discussed, the objects or activities to be described. The title is the label given to your speech for the purpose of arousing the audience's interest. The title is a sort of advertising slogan which dresses up your subject in an attractive form.

Your title should be relevant, that is, it should have something to do with the subject or with some part of your discussion of it. The title should always be brief. And it should be provocative without being controversial. If the audience are in any way hostile to your purpose you must not let that purpose be too obvious in your title.

Making an outline

While you will make a rough sketch of your speech before you collect the material for it you cannot prepare an outline until your material is actually to hand. With this information you will set down first of all the main points you expect to make and the order in which you will make them. The opening and closing paragraphs should always be written out in full.

This outline will be a type of skeleton or blueprint to be filled in later, and it will merely indicate the presentation's structure. You should allow for each main point to be well supported by facts, examples, and illustrations. It need hardly be said that a speech on the occasion of the retirement of the secretary of your cricket club to be given in your 'local' will not have such an elaborate outline; the following is intended for a more formal occasion.

I. Specific Purpose Statement and Introduction
II. Main Statement
    (a) sub-point
       (1) Supporting fact
       (2) Supporting illustration
    (b) sub-point
       (1) Example
       (2) Example
       (3) Detail
III. Second Main Statement
IV. Third Main Statement
    (a) sub-point
       (1) Supporting details

(2)   Supporting details
    (b)   sub-point
V.   Conclusion

Having done all this, your next step will be to clothe the outline with as many words as will recall to your mind the development of each main point. Key words will often do—but some statistics cannot be committed to memory. Remember that your words should be such as will really bring to mind the thoughts you want to put across.

Immediate preparation

Now you have your outline you should practice going over the presentation aloud once or twice, or more if you need to. But avoid reciting it on too many occasions, otherwise it will become stale. Practice making your manner of speaking seem personal. Get the family to listen if possible.

Your experience, ability and knowledge of your subject will determine how much practising you need to do, and don't worry about leaving bits of it out the first time you go over it. Just add a few more key words to your outline and go over it again. Don't be alarmed if the presentation never seems the same from one session to another—it will always be somewhat different each time. This is good, because you won't then be alarmed on the occasion of giving the talk if once again it is a little different. This may well reflect your mood of the moment. In fact, even when you have given your talk you should feel you have left some good points out completely and could kick yourself for doing so! That's a sign you had ample material and you should be encouraged by it.

For any formal presentation outside my normal day-to-day involvement I always try to sneak a look at the hall or room where I am going to speak, and, if possible, stand for a few minutes at the rostrum. This gives me 'the feel' of the place and an idea of how I need to project my voice if no microphone is being provided. I find this helps even if it's only an hour or so before the talk, because when I do begin I have that comforting feeling that I'm not a complete stranger to my surroundings.

I suggest you try to find out if anyone is going to leave before your talk is over. I remember the first seminar I gave on effective speaking. It was in a large London hotel with about two dozen in attendance. I had been speaking for an hour when one rather distinguished looking individual gathered all his papers together, put them in his briefcase, stood up and strode out of the room. I was absolutely shattered. It ruined the remainder of my session. I kept trying to concentrate on my material and at the same time kept wondering what on earth I did to offend him. Could I possibly be that poor a lecturer? As it turned out, the Course Administrator had forgotten to tell me that this delegate had asked to be excused to attend a Board Meeting. He returned later in the day and was a pleasant and an excellent participant throughout the remaining sessions.

Another acquaintance of mine was addressing a local political meeting and noticed to his dismay just as he was nearing the conclusion of his talk that a number of ladies at the front of the audience got up and left. As it turned out they were only going to make the inevitable cup of tea for everybody. But in the meantime it affected the conclusion of his talk. The moral of these stories is—always ask the chairman if anyone is expected to leave before the end of the meeting. Even if he says 'no' and some still do leave, don't be overly concerned. There's probably a simple explanation for it. But if half your audience leaves then I would suppose, if I were you, that perhaps something had gone slightly wrong!

As our suggested outline above showed, your presentation should consist of three main parts: (a) an introduction; (b) a body; and (c) a conclusion. Obvious enough, you may say, but I have listened to several talks where these three parts were difficult to distinguish from one another and where I became suspicious that they did not in fact exist in recognizable form! The secret of good speaking is to get a good introduction, a good conclusion, and keep them as close together as possible.

The introduction of a presentation is difficult, as the minds of your audience are fresh and comparatively easy to impress at that stage, and it therefore is highly important. Your introduction should always be worked out carefully in advance. Inexperienced speakers often take far too much liberty in talking at length before their listeners know the subject to be considered.

You should therefore announce your subject or remind the group of the point being considered at the outset. This should be well lodged in your mind from your specific purpose statement (SPS). What do you want to achieve in your talk? What is the message you want to get across? Is it to inform, to instruct or to persuade? Be as specific as you can in your answer to this because if you are not able to define precisely the object of the exercise you cannot help but give a waffly presentation. The SPS is for your own use, however, and need not, indeed should not, always be disclosed to your audience. You would not say, for example, 'I'm going to persuade you to buy my company's products from now on'. You must be tactful and courteous, especially if you are going to be controversial.

Your introduction should be short. Never apologise for speaking. Do not assume that you must begin every speaking session with a joke or humorous anecdote. Most people are not naturally funny, and you may find that the lack of hilarious laughter is a bit off-putting to say the least. Only if you have a rare gift for humour should you introduce it at the beginning, otherwise the effect will usually be to embarrass the audience rather than entertain them. If you feel you really must, for some reason, begin with a funny story then at least make sure it is completely relevant to your subject, and don't drag some story in by the ears just to be funny.

Never begin with that ghastly expression 'I'd like to say a few words about . . .'. Most people whom I have heard begin in this manner have done just that! They have said a few unco-ordinated, disjointed, badly chosen words which had a disastrous effect on their audience.

You can often open your talk by asking the audience a direct or rhetorical question. You may state some shocking fact: 'The number of murders committed in this city every year amounts to one every twenty-five minutes.' You can use a well-known quotation. For business presentations probably the most effective opening is to show how your listeners will be richer, more effective, fatter, thinner, happier or will live longer if they give what you are about to say their serious consideration. The important thing is to establish audience interest (and sympathy) from the start. The more natural and informal the beginning, the better.

If your subject is really of vital interest to your audience you can often merely state it and plunge right in to the subject. If you were addressing undergraduates, for example, you might begin by saying 'I am going to talk with you about good jobs, how to get them and then how to keep them'. At an anniversary, annual dinner or dedication ceremony it will be sufficient to refer to the occasion itself.

Few things put an audience off more than an overbearing and pompous speaker. A brief, friendly, businesslike introduction is the correct way to begin any talk.

Don't begin a talk by apologising for your presence (although you can apologise for some indisposition such as a cold or cough), and do not begin with that awful worn-out phrase 'Unaccustomed as I am . . .' Often you may refer to the remarks of the person who introduces you or you may refer to what has been said by a previous speaker. This is particularly advisable when the previous speaker has created a good impression which you want to build upon, even if you find it necessary to oppose him later in your own talk.

Above all, your introduction should be elegant, that is, it should be marked by careful and tasteful selection and execution, and should have refinement, finish and simplicity.

The conclusion

In one sense the close of any talk is its most strategic element. What is said last is likely to be remembered longest. The ending should be the last blow of the hammer on the nail you have been banging throughout your speech. The conclusion has to be most carefully planned, and you should know it by heart word for word. This will give you a little extra confidence throughout, because as you speak you will know you won't have to struggle to find an effective ending. The end of a talk is rather like the sweet after dinner—we expect one, and if it is good we are inclined to remember the whole meal with pleasure.

Hints on your conclusion

Never end with an apology for going overtime—never *go* overtime. Don't say 'Well that's about all I have to say on the subject so I'll conclude now'. Stop, but don't talk about stopping. The end of your presentation should convey a sense of completeness and finality. Round off your talk and do not leave it broken and rough like a jagged rock. If, towards the end of your ordeal, you do say 'finally' then please make sure you mean it! Don't make the mistake of saying 'finally' and later say 'in conclusion' adding later for good measure 'my last point is' and 'I want to repeat again' ending up with 'it only remains for me to say'! If you say it is your last point then there should be no going back. Your audience will become restless and feel cheated as you keep re-kindling the hope each time that you really mean you are near the end.

I have also known people to run overtime, panic and sit down forgetting even to propose the resolution which was the sole object of their speech!

Some ways of ending a talk

The following are five suggested ways of ending any speech.

Appealing for action

This method is a definite and emphatic appeal to take a specific course of action or to feel or believe in some particular way. But there is a danger in its being used too often by amateur speakers who feel that action must always be the result of speech. Let us have a look at two examples of this type of ending. The first is based on the noble dictates of conscience. It is the close of Lord Brougham's appeal in the House of Lords, in 1838, for the emancipation of negro slaves.

'So now the fullness of time is come for the discharging of our duty to the African captive ... The time has come, the trial has been made, the hour is striking; you have no longer a pretext for hesitation, or faltering, or delay. The slave has shown, by four years' blameless behaviour and devotion to the pursuits of peaceful industry, that he is as fit for his freedom as any English peasant, aye, or any Lord whom I now address. I demand his rights; I demand his liberty without stint. In the name of justice and of law, in the name of reason, in the name of God, who has given you no right to work injustice, I demand that your brother be no longer trampled upon as your slave! I make my appeal to the Commons, who represent the free people of England, and I require at their hands the performance of that condition for which they paid so enormous a price—that condition which all their constituents are in breathless anxiety to see fulfilled! I appeal to this House! Hereditary judges of the first tribunal in the world, to you I appeal for justice! Patrons of all the arts that humanise mankind, under your protection I place humanity itself! To the merciful Sovereign of a free people, I call aloud for mercy to the hundreds of thousands for whom half a million of her Christian sisters have cried out; I ask that their cry may not have risen in vain. But, first, I turn my eye to the Throne of all justice, and devoutly humbling myself before Him who is of purer eyes than to behold such vast iniquities, I implore that the curse hovering over the head of the unjust and the oppressor be averted from us, that your hearts may be turned to mercy, and that over all the earth His will may at length be done!'

It is unlikely that you or I will ever have to deliver such a discourse in such surroundings, but the speech is an interesting study of the means by which an effective orator plays upon the emotions and beliefs of his audience in order to call for action. He is not calling for agreement but for decisive action, and he does so in an indirect way.

The second example concerns matters with which you and I are more likely to be involved—municipal affairs.

> 'Ladies and Gentlemen: The City Engineer has placed in the hands of each of you the detailed plans for improving the purity of our water supply; he has shown that the safety of our children and the health of our entire city demand the approval of these plans; the decision can no longer be delayed. I ask you to appropriate the necessary funds.'

Summarizing, re-stating or outlining briefly the main points you have covered

In a speech where you are imparting information this ending is usually the best. For all normal commercial presentations I prefer this type of conclusion to all others provided you do not tell the audience you are going to give a recapitulation of all the main points you have already made. Make sure that you do not introduce new ideas in the guise of your summary or embellish thoughts that have appeared in the body of your speech.

Even if you speak for only five minutes your listeners are apt to be a little hazy about your precise points. They have become crystal clear in your own mind because you have been pondering over them for some time but they may all be new to the audience. The summary ending means that they have little excuse for being like Iago seeming 'to remember a mass of things but nothing distinctly'!

Pay the audience a sincere compliment

You can just say how attentive they have been and that you would like to express your thanks for their kind hospitality. The following could be suitable: 'Ladies and Gentlemen, it has been a delight to be with you. I hope that my words will have been of some help in promoting the cause for which you work and in which I—like you—believe in firmly. I wish you, Mr Chairman, your honorary officers, council, members and workers, every possible success in your great venture.' There must be no gross flattery or extravagance. Your complimentary ending must be sincere, otherwise it will ring very, very false.

Use a quotation

If you do use a quotation at the end of your talk it must bear directly on your central idea and suggest the attitude or action you want taken. A businessman might quote some economic axiom or important recent pronouncement. There are dozens of good books available containing thousands of quotations on varied subjects. Every speaker should have, for example, a copy of *The Oxford Dictionary of Quotations*. When you do use a quotation make sure it is correct and don't use one from Chaucer and attribute it to Shakespeare.

Use an anecdote

If you can effectively conclude by leaving your audience laughing this should be done—provided always the occasion is a suitable one for laughter. Humour should arise naturally from the subject matter. Any joke should be signalled and it must be appropriate to the audience as well as to the occasion. If you are concluding with a joke, do get the story right. We have all seen people get hopelessly involved half-way because some vital point was missed, or because the 'punch line' was given right at the beginning.

Many of the best stories are those told about oneself, and original anecdotes are often very interesting. But don't take 'the one about' story and pretend it happened to you personally. Never laugh at your own jokes and never tell an obscene story. Whatever the occasion may be, this rule will save you and your audience much embarrassment, and they will hold you in higher esteem in the long run because of it.

Having concluded, do not slink surreptitiously into your seat but sit down slowly to the pleasant sound of well-earned applause!

Impromptu speaking

When you are invited to a convivial gathering there is often the chance that you will be called upon to 'say a few words'. My advice up to now has been—don't! But there may well be occasions when it would be discourteous or for some reason impossible to refuse. My suggestion is that you always go along to such occasions with a few appropriate notes on a 3 in × 5 in card in your pocket. You can then quietly produce these if called upon to speak and do a reasonably commendable job. People do not judge impromptu speeches as strictly as those where preparation is expected to have been done.

If you do get stuck for something to say on a subject here are a few suggested ways of organizing your thoughts and which should help you speak reasonably coherently.

Date sequence

Begin at a certain period in time and move forward or backward from that. Do not reverse the order once you have begun nor jumble the dates. This sequence is particularly good when your purpose is to give information.

Space sequence

Here you can arrange your material from east to west or north to south. You could discuss the density of population according to geographical areas, or the plans of a building could be considered floor by floor.

Cause and effect sequence

This order may be used in speeches to persuade. In describing certain conditions and events you can prove that certain forces created them.

Problem-solution sequence

On many occasions your material can be divided into two major sections: the description of a problem or related problems and the presentation of solutions. This sequence is normally used in reference to problems which are actually facing your audience, or future problems that will arise if things go on as they are or are planned at the present. It is particularly suitable for community situations and opposition to official schemes for the local area, where everyone present is expected to make his or her contribution.

Points for discussion

What are the five generally accepted steps in remote preparation?

What is the difference between a presentation given in chronological order and one given in spatial order? In what circumstances would you use each? (AIA)

What suggestions do you have for a speaker on the selecting and narrowing of the subject matter?

Draw up an outline for a talk on Pollution to the local Rotary Club.

Draft a short talk which, as Personnel Officer, you would give to a small group of new junior employees on time-keeping. (ICSA)

Why is the summary at the end of a talk considered by most to be the correct way to end?

6 Delivery

'There is perhaps no greater hardship at present inflicted on mankind in civilized and free countries than the necessity of listening to someone else'

Anthony Trollope

Having prepared thoroughly what you are going to say your next task is obviously to say it. Many feel that the way something is said is more important than what is said. I'm not one of them. But I do feel it is *almost* as important a factor because in oral communication people see as well as hear.

When you are called upon to speak there will usually be applause. You should time your getting up just so that it coincides with the tail end of the applause. Then wait. Wait for about four or five seconds before beginning. The amateur always rushes in before the audience have really had time to mentally absorb the fact that he's there. Give your audience time to be quiet, and during that few seconds don't glare at them—just look out over them and smile.

Dress

I don't know of any occasion on which you will be expected to speak to a group of people without wearing clothes! For most speaking situations formal dress is required. If in any doubt about what you should wear ask the chairman in advance, although in cases such as an after-dinner speech formal dress is usually required. In the U.S. a questionnaire was sent to a large group of people by a psychologist and university president, asking them the impression clothes made on them. Almost unanimously, they testified that when they were well groomed and attired, the knowledge of it, the feeling of it, had an effect which while it was difficult to explain, was still very definite, very real. It gave them more confidence, brought them increased faith in themselves and heightened their self-respect.

Anything bizarre or outlandish should be avoided, as your personal appearance should be as neat, pleasing and unobtrusive as possible. You need not be expensively dressed, but your clothing needs to be pleasing to the eye. New suits or footwear should not generally be worn

34

as you cannot fully feel at ease in items that have not as yet become a part of you. Neatness in dress gives the impression that your mind is as well ordered and normal as your clothes. Be careful that there is nothing about your dress which looks clumsy such as bulging pockets, and don't have a galaxy of pens showing from your jacket pocket.

Eye contact

As mentioned earlier, eye contact with your audience is of immense importance. This does not mean staring or glaring at your listeners, but looking them all directly in the eye from time to time. Be sure you don't have a 'blind' side when you speak; spread your attention over all sections of the audience equally. You do not have to peer into people's eyes, but by swinging your gaze over every section of the room you will give each person the feeling that you are talking to him or her. Quite apart from the fact that it is only polite to look at your audience, you will be able to judge from the reactions you see whether or not you are getting your message across, and can adjust the number of points you wish to make in any situation accordingly. In a small or informal group such as a number of employees in the office you will be able to ask one of them who appears a bit mystified if you have said something with which he disagrees or does not understand.

Only by having good direct eye contact with the audience will you be able to sense the effect your talk is having, and at the same time make sure your audience feel you are talking to them personally. Know the content of your speech so well that you do not have to spend all your mental energy remembering the sequence of your ideas but can concentrate more on your audience.

Posture

The next thing to do is to adopt the proper stance. Your posture should be quiet and comfortable without being slouchy. It should be erect but not stiff—don't stand to attention with your heels together. Your feet should be comfortably apart but beware of the widespread legs of a sailor in a bad storm or the posture of the Colossus at Rhodes. Stand on the balls of your feet with the toes gripping the floor, but do not jiggle up and down. Your bearing should give the impression that you are in command of yourself and the situation—which should, in fact, be the case in your everyday posture even if you never spoke a word in public.

The next problem is what to do with your hands, which suddenly may seem enormous. If they feel like a bunch of bananas to you don't be deluded into imagining that anyone else is paying the slightest attention to them or has the slightest interest in them. It is best to keep them out of your pockets, but don't put them on your hips as if you are about to perform gymnastic tricks. Nor should you clasp your lapels like some politician or television barrister!

One valuable use of notes is that you have something to do with your hands. Many people try to lean forward on a table or hide behind a stand so that their hands are not loose. This is useless. Your hands should really occupy several positions throughout your presentation: by your side, behind your back, holding your notes, and gesturing, about which we have more to say presently.

Movement

Movement and gestures become more important as the size of your audience increases. In the case of the small group the hearers are close to you and can see the least change in your facial expression and the slightest movement of your hands and body. Thus they are able to make up their minds easily as to just how you feel about what you are saying. But in the case of the large group your audience are so far away that a good deal of your facial expressions and smaller movements of the hands and body are lost. Consequently your movements should be more expansive—you must 'write large' your response to your thoughts.

One effect of movement is to attract your hearers' attention—the eye instinctively follows moving objects and focuses upon them. So long as your movement is natural and easy this is valuable, but you must be careful that it does not become a distraction to the audience. Don't stride up and down while talking like the American lawyer in the television court-room scenes; nor should you prance aimlessly about.

Transitions from one point to another may be indicated by a lateral movement of just a step or two. Such a movement is literally a signal that 'I am finished with that point; now let us turn our attention to another'. Always start lateral movements with the foot that is on the side toward which you are going (that is, your right foot if you move to the right) in order to avoid awkwardly crossing your feet, and then walk just a step or two in that direction. Forward or backward movements usually serve to imply the degree of importance attached to an idea. A step forward indicates that you are coming to a more important point which you do not wish your hearers to miss. Backward movement suggests that you are willing for them to relax a bit to let the last idea take root before you present another important point.

In general, the more formal the occasion the fewer your movements should be; and the larger the audience, the more steps you should take when you do move. If you avoid the extremes of remaining glued to the position or being on the move all the time your natural impulses will take care of the rest.

Gestures

In our everyday conversation we all gesture freely. A gesture is merely an action of the body to convey some thought or emotion, or to reinforce any oral expression. So it should be natural for us, when addressing a group, to have some gestures to give life to our speaking. By gestures I do not mean fidgeting with buttons, watches or papers: I mean purposeful expressions. Most of us gesture far too infrequently when we address a group of people, so we must practise it while we practise our speaking until the gesturing becomes spontaneous. Never write down in your notes, for example, 'gesture at this point'—the gesture will be stilted and probably ill-timed. We do not react 'piecemeal' to any situation—the whole human body is present in any reaction, so our gestures should be free flowing and not artificial or theatrical. The impulse to gesture must come from within rather than without.

Gestures have a three-fold value: they assist in the communication of your ideas, they increase your energy and self-confidence and they hold your audience's attention. To achieve this they need to be reasonably vigorous so that they are convincing. They need to be definite—not, for instance, pointing only in the general direction of something but pointing at some specific object in a drawing or other aid. And they need to be properly timed. The gesture's stroke should fall right on or slightly before the point it is used to emphasize.

Let's just consider some normal and natural gestures in brief. These can easily be employed in most speaking situations.

When advising caution or when you are asking for very careful consideration (which, incidentally, implies a slower rate of delivery and slower thinking among your audience), extend your arms to the audience, with hands pressed back towards the wrists and palms showing to the audience.

If a cat with dirty paws were to jump up on your clean clothes, you would push it down and to one side with your hand. In the same way you can express your disapproval, or rejection, of an idea. This movement with the palm of the hand turned down can be used to reinforce such statements as 'That proposal is absolutely useless' or 'It can't be done that way'.

An obvious gesture occasionally useful in expressing strong opposition to an idea is the raising to shoulder height of the clenched fist. By contrast, in expressing welcome, extend the arms as if in embrace.

By moving your hand from side to side with the palm held vertically, you can indicate the separation of facts or ideas into different parts. You might, for instance, appropriately use this gesture while saying 'We must be neither radical in our ideas nor ultraconservative'—moving your hand to one side on the word 'radical' and to the other on the word 'conservative'.

The above are given just to show what can be done—gestures are a very personal item, should always be employed but never over-used.

Voice

Pitch your voice so that the people at the back of the room can hear you. If you have a microphone this will present little problem, but do realize that microphones are sensitive objects and don't spit at them, pummel them or treat them roughly. It should be tested before you begin: if not, just say 'one, two, three, testing', or something like that to see if the people can all hear you. But be prepared for the microphone to break down and don't be alarmed if it does—you will just have to put on more power. This has happened to me several times and unfortunate though it is, where the group is one hundred or less, I have just had to continue.

I feel it is a good idea to ask those at the back of the group if they can hear you. Many feel this is not a good idea, but I consider that it is much better to establish this fact fairly near the beginning of your address than to have someone shout 'speak up mate' when you are half-way through! But there is no necessity to ask this where you are the fourth speaker, there is a microphone and everyone else has heard the previous speakers perfectly. It is only where you genuinely feel there may be a difficulty that you should ask this question.

In your delivery do nothing to dull your natural energy—it is natural and it is magnetic, and one of the greatest assets any speaker can employ.

Points for discussion

Why is correct dress important while giving a presentation?

It is very important for a speaker to maintain contact with his audience. How do you suggest this be achieved? (InstAA)

Do you consider mannerisms should be employed while communicating to a group of people?

How would you physically indicate transitions in your talk from one point to another?

What do you consider to be a good platform manner for the public speaker? (InstAA)

7 Using Visual Aids

'Every man is born with the faculty of reason and the faculty of speech, but why should he be able to speak before he has anything to say?'

Benjamin Whitecote

In any presentation you are making, if your listeners use more than one sense to receive your message, they have a better chance of remembering what you have said. Visual aids also assist the memory and give variety to a talk. A very brief sub-division of aids would be:

(a) symbolic or actual;
(b) two-dimensional or three-dimensional.

With all your visual aids the aims should be simplicity and clarity. Always prepare, so that you will know precisely how your illustrations will work out and the timing of their use.

We sometimes forget that visual aids have their disadvantages as well as their advantages. They cost money, take up a fair amount of time and thought and, for someone who makes very few presentations, they diminish flexibility. If they go wrong they invariably cause a certain amount of embarrassment and confusion. The number of times I have seen them go wrong is almost astronomical! My advice is to go prepared to deliver your talk if everything breaks down, and then you will at least avoid total disaster.

In any case you should always ask the question—can we manage just as well without them? Films, slides, epidiascopes and blackboards all have their place, but they should be kept firmly in it! They are *aids* not crutches. Besides this they should be visual and not visual verbals; they should not be just words written out on slides or charts, unless you are develping a complicated argument which may need headings or reminders of important points revealed one at a time. People often put words on slides and then proceed to read them off as though they were talking to children of young school age—don't do this. Your audience are quite capable of reading.

Symbolic or actual aids
When you use one object to represent another, you are using a symbolic

visual aid. Surprisingly, this can often be more effective than the real thing. You can indicate size by using familiar objects such as pens, books, tables, or the room itself. Because your listeners frequently see such objects, they have a clear picture of what you are talking about; whereas they may seldom see the real object itself. You can use the objects in an average room to show size, shape and colour as well as texture. For example, you can show how the size of a component has decreased by comparing its original size with a book and its present size with a coin. Another general point arises here which is that we should always relate the unknown to the known even when we are not using visual aids. It is pointless to talk to a group of non-business people about millions of pounds, or cubic capacity, etc., without relating it to something with which they are in daily contact and can readily comprehend.

The other method is to show the object itself. If you talk about a transistor, then show one; if you are talking about some material, show a sample. If you can get your audience to hear and see what you are putting over or even to feel or smell it you will obviously make a much deeper impression. A picture is worth a thousand words.

Two-dimensional aids
These can be static or moving. Static aids include blackboards, flip-charts, flannel-boards, magnetic boards and projectors. Projectors can also provide moving visual aids.

Blackboards
Although blackboards are often considered old-fashioned, they still provide one of the best means of presenting two-dimensional visual aids. Their big disadvantage is that chalk (even the 'dust-free' variety) is usually very dusty and messy.

However, they are particularly useful for diagrams, key-words, or sketches. They have the following advantages:

(1) you can rub out mistakes, or modify your picture, as you present your talk;

(2) you can prepare your material beforehand or build it up as you go along.

An experienced speaker or lecturer plans his diagrams beforehand even if he is going to draw them as he goes along. A piece of quarto paper is roughly proportional to most blackboards, so this makes it useful for roughing out what you intend to put on the blackboard. If you don't do this, your sketches may look a bit muddled. Don't mix the use of a blackboard with slides or film kits—wait until all of them have been shown before you use the blackboard.

Yellow chalk shows up better than white, and a damp duster or sponge should be used in preference to a dry one. You can draw your lines or circles beforehand on the blackboard if you want to and these will be invisible to the audience. As you chalk them over during your talk you will have a crisp and professional result. Any lettering should be large enough to be seen easily at the other end of the room. Complex material should always be avoided; portray the main idea as simply as possible. Make it vivid so that it is easily remembered. Colour can be used to great effect. When you use a blackboard, don't spend too much time writing on it or talking to it—look at your listeners. (When pointing to the board stay on the same side and point with your left hand so that you are facing your audience).

If you are right-handed, the board should be on your left as you face the audience so that you obscure much less of it when you are drawing. If there is sufficient room plan to start drawing one third of the way across, using only the far two thirds, and you will obscure less still. If you are using a pointer don't wave it vaguely around the board or the room. Just point precisely at what you are discussing, leave it there motionless, then take it away.

Flip-charts

These are large sheets of cheap (newsprint-type) paper, usually clipped to boards. Coloured inks or crayons are used to draw on them. Like a blackboard, a flip-chart can be prepared beforehand or built up as you proceed. Different stages can be shown on different sheets, which can be placed on top of each other, so that each can be un-covered at the appropriate time. The great advantage of flip-charts is that they eliminate chalk dust. However, you cannot rub out if you make a mistake. If you do make an error the best thing is to scrap the particular sheet and start again on a fresh one. Flip-charts should not be over-used; too many of them only distract your audience.

Both flip-charts and blackboards can be used for charts and graphs including:

organization charts   network diagrams
cut-away diagrams   bar charts
line graphs   pie charts
maps

Sheets should preferably be perforated or on rings. If they are not, they are liable to start falling back on you about a third of the way through your discourse. Keep all charts, graphs, diagrams, etc., simple and clear. Putting too much material on visual aids is probably the commonest fault of all. Use heavy broad lines and plenty of colour. Omit unnecessary details. A series of simple charts is much better than a single complicated one.

Use the visual aid at the proper psychological point in the speech. If the timing is off the chain of thought will be broken, and the visual aids will serve only to break the continuity of your presentation instead of clarifying a point.

Flannel-boards and magnetic boards

Flannel-boards are boards covered with felt, or a similar substance. Diagrams or lettering backed with felt can be placed on them and will remain in position until removed. They are fairly expensive, and the material has normally to be prepared beforehand, but they are useful when the same presentation has to be given a number of times. Magnetic boards are similar to flannel-boards but they have a magnetic surface, and small pieces of metal are used as a backing to hold the figures to the board. Sometimes the metal itself can be cut to shape and used as it is instead of as a backing for paper, etc. Sometimes a magnetic board has a surface which can be used as a blackboard as well. Both of these are useful for bar, line, or pie graphs.

Slides

I can honestly say that in my entire business experience I have seen only about two or three presentations using slides where there has not been some mishap either humanly induced or through some failure in the machinery. Indeed I have seen many where several things went wrong all at once and I've even been present where the sense of disaster increased from beginning to end!

All slide presentations should be approached with the utmost care and attention. For such presentations one normally uses a 35 mm projector and the small slides can be purchased in advance or made quite simply with the aid of a 35 mm camera. Ready-made slides are recommended wherever possible as they are usually of first class quality although it may be difficult to buy slides which fit your requirements exactly.

When you propose to use slides (or films), elementary though it may seem, you must make sure that a projector will be available and in good working order. If you are using your own, check that the electricity supply, plugs and length of cable are suitable. If you have to set up the show yourself, remember to arrive in plenty of time. It is absolutely essential that you rehearse at least twice beforehand (preferably in front of someone with a stop watch). If you want to provide a reasonably large picture the projector will need to be several yards away from you which will make it likely that you will not be able to control the projector yourself. If you can control it you should always do so but if this is not possible (for example if the cable is not long enough) you will need the help of a qualified intelligent projectionist. I have seen several presentations ruined because the speaker and the projectionist misunderstood each other and there was a severe lack between them of 'the peace which passeth all understanding'! So you need to rehearse the presentation *together* and you must have an agreed word or sign—which cannot be misunderstood—as a signal that the slide needs changing. Make sure the slides are the right way up and the right way round which can easily be done by means of an identifying mark on each.

One advantage of having a projectionist is that this allows you to give full attention to your audience. But once again remember that your projectionist must have a thorough knowledge of your script and indeed he should have a copy beside him (plus a torch) as you work your way through it. If, incidentally, a slide is required twice make two copies and never try to lift one out and insert in a different place. They are very small (only about $1\frac{1}{2}'' \times 1\frac{1}{2}''$), very light and have a habit of falling under ledges, pieces of paper, etc., which is another reason for the torch. If the choice is yours do pick a projectionist who will not panic and work out a breakdown procedure with him just in case something does go wrong, go wrong, go wrong. . .

As far as the slides themselves are concerned there is one vital question you must ask yourself: what will they *show*—not what will they *say*. You are supposed to be the talker, not the slides. Few things are more boring to look at than slides which have just one or two words on them. What the slides do show they should show clearly. All too many people try to cram too much on to one slide thereby making absolutely certain that those sitting at the back cannot for the life of them make out what the slide is supposed to detail. If you have too much material or detail for one slide have a series of two or three instead. Your slide should not be too complex with charts, figures, arrows and boxes filling the square completely. People cannot concentrate on what you are saying if they are desperately trying to figure what some complex slide is supposed to show. And if you have to do the explaining when each slide comes up the presentation will go on for ever. Just make your slides simple and uncrowded and this can be achieved by using a series rather than trying to cram everything on to one or two.

One of the features which make slides and films so attractive to audiences is that they can contain colour and this is a factor to make use of when preparing your slide presentation. Don't produce drab black and white ones if colour can be used to good effect.

Never hold a slide up for too long. The attention should be on you and when the slide has served its purpose remove it immediately. You would hardly think it necessary to mention this (and I wouldn't if I had not seen it happen so often) but do explain each slide. Don't put a slide up and continue muttering away with only a passing reference to it. People will be wondering why on earth it is being shown and their attention will wander from you, the speaker.

If you (or your company) do not have your own slides or photographs or film strips there are various organizations which hire projection equipment and machinery. Some Government Departments and Local Authorities can also be extremely helpful in this. Last of all, you should go prepared to give your talk without any slides at all; then if a power failure or some other minor catastrophe occurs you can carry on in a reasonably coherent manner. I do not want to be unduly pessimistic but good slide presentations are few and far between and they require a great deal of practice. Remember Murphy's law says that anything which *can* go wrong *will* go wrong. Like O'Reilly I tend to feel Murphy was really an incurable optimist!

Overhead projectors

Overhead projectors which are operated by the speaker are becoming increasingly popular not only in colleges and universities but also in the business environment. They are a very versatile piece of equipment and have the advantage over slide presentations that they have a powerful light source which requires little if any dimming of the light in the room where they are being used provided the screen is in a slightly darkened corner. They also have a short throw which means the speaker can always control their operation.

The transparencies themselves can be prepared by hand and some are made up of several leaves of acetate so that by putting one sheet on top of another, each having additional information or drawings, a most useful effect can be produced.

But once again you must ensure that your plates are in the right order, the right way up and the right way round and you must not keep watching the screen behind you or your audience won't hear clearly what you are trying to say. Most overhead projectors now in use also have the facility to use a roll of clear acetate which may be pulled across the platen of the machine by the speaker using a small handle at the side. This can then be used in place of a blackboard (it is possible to erase anything written or drawn in error) and it gives you the advantage of being able to face your audience as you write instead of having your back to them as you do when using a blackboard.

Ensure that the light is not switched on until your plate is in position and that it is switched off before it is moved away. With the warning that this, as all pieces of machinery used in business presentations, should be approached with a healthy respect I thoroughly recommend it as a visual aid.

Points for discussion

'A picture is worth a thousand words'. Explain with examples the meaning of this statement. (ICSA)

Give a few examples of two-dimensional aids.

Why are blackboards still considered useful in the context of visual aids?

What points should one consider specifically when using slides during a business presentation?

What are the main advantages and disadvantages in using a projector and slides in any presentation? (AIA)

8 Selection Interviewing

'There is no index of character so sure as the voice'

Disraeli

The selection of a suitable individual for a job presents several different kinds of problem. First among these is the setting out of the demands of the job in terms of the personal qualities which must be displayed to carry it out successfully. Secondly comes the recognition of these qualities in the short space of time which can be allocated to an interview. Thirdly, there is the conducting of the interview so that the evidence for an assessment of these qualities becomes available.

Setting out the demands of a job

Job analysis is the term used to describe the study of jobs. For repetitive tasks the techniques of work-study can be used, while for those of a non-repetitive nature, activity sampling can produce a description of the various elements of which they are made up. Once the analysis has been completed a Job Description can be drawn up which presents a complete and systematic account of what the job involves. This can be set out under a series of headings such as: *Title of job. Position in the Organization* (showing to whom the occupier of the post is responsible, those who are responsible to him, his horizontal links, and so forth). *Duties and Responsibilities*. This covers the results by which the occupier will be judged, the objectives he is expected to achieve, and a series of key tasks which must be carried out within a specific time. In this area it should be possible to lay down quantitative standards, such as for output, quality, cost recovery and so on. *Working Conditions*, with specific reference to any factors in the physical environment, working hours, etc., which may vary from the normal. *Economic Conditions*, covering rates of remuneration, fringe benefits, conditions of service, etc.

Once the Job Description has been completed we must consider the personal qualities required in the individual. This has been referred to as the Job Specification by some writers, by others as the Man Specification and by others as the Personnel Specification. Whatever term may be used, it is important to remember that we have now moved away from a description of a job to a specification of a person. The Personnel

Specification sets out the kind of person who is likely to do the job effectively, and in many ways presents greater difficulties than merely describing a job.

Prominent among these difficulties are the problems of vocabulary. We lack a series of terms which are precise and objective to describe the attributes of an individual. Those which are in common use may mean one thing to one person and something quite different to another. Moreover, they are nearly always evaluative, that is, they convey an attitude of approval or disapproval. This tends to confuse the issue, for the qualities which are 'good' in one situation may be 'bad' in another. What we need, therefore, is a framework of terms which are precise and objective, and which are non-evaluative, as a means of specifying the kind of person required for any job with which we are concerned.

Five-fold framework

This is provided by the Five-Fold Framework described below.

Impact

We are first concerned with the kind of impact which the individual makes on other people. This is determined by his appearance and dress, his speech and manner, and most important of all, his self-confidence in dealing with other people. These may be superficial qualities, but they are the ones which determine the kind of reaction which the individual calls out from others. And in certain jobs this reaction may be of a major significance in success. A salesman, for example, no matter how well qualified he may be in the technical sense, must be able to establish contact quickly with a new prospect and must be able to build up the kind of relationship which will enable him to present his product to the best advantage. Similarly, many management jobs and positions of a supervisory nature involve continual contact with other people, and unless the individual has the kind of manner which can draw out favourable reactions he will be under a handicap.

It is important, therefore, to consider a job from this point of view quite separately and to make up our minds about its demands.

When considering individuals it is also important to keep this separate. Many decisions are influenced far more than people realize by this aspect of personality. Thus, anyone who can put himself forward effectively, express himself with confidence and make a good initial impression, may receive more consideration than his other personal qualities really justify. Conversely, those who lack self-confidence, who find difficulty in expressing themselves, and who lack sensitivity to the reactions of others, may be overlooked, even though their other personal qualities may be more impressive.

Qualifications

Qualifications cover the next aspect to be considered, and comprise the individual's general education, his technical training and his work experience. These present little difficulty in practice, for objective standards are available in examinations, certificates, membership of professional bodies, and so on. We can lay out general education, for example, in terms of the Certificate of Secondary Education, G.C.E. 'O' and 'A' levels or University degrees. Similarly we can set out technical training in terms of City and Guilds Certificates, Ordinary National or Higher National Certificates. Experience can also be set out in terms of so many years in this level of job, or so many in that level. There are few problems of judgment here in this area, for if we have decided that a job calls for a Higher National Certificate in Mechanical Engineering then an applicant has either got it or he has not got it. The decision thus makes itself, so that while this aspect may be important in effective selection, it is comparatively simple and straightforward.

Innate abilities

Everyday observation makes it clear that there are differences in 'quickness on the uptake'. Some people have the kind of mind that can take in everything that is said to them and make the kind of responses that show that they have understood it and are ready for the next step. Other people have slow minds, and need to have a thing explained several times before one can be sure they have taken it in. These differences show up in intelligence tests, and can play a part in the kind of job for which they are fitted. Brains by themselves, however, are not everything, for it is the use that an individual makes of his abilities that really determines how far he gets. This leads on to the next aspect.

Motivation

Motivation is the term used to describe the kind of goals an individual sets for himself, his consistency in following them up, his initiative in overcoming difficulties, and his effectiveness in achieving results in action. This is the heading that plays the most important part in an individual's success at work and consequently it is the one to which we should be paying most attention in selection. Different jobs make different demands from this point of view, while individuals have different endowments. Some people can be successful in jobs which call for a great deal of drive and energy, which others are much happier in the kind of routine post which only involves carrying out the same round of duties day after day. It is a matter of supreme importance that we should be clear about the demands of the job from this point of view and also about the potentialities of the individual.

Adjustment

Our final heading covers the emotional side of personality. This shows most obviously in the amount of stress an individual can take. Here again we are confronted with differences, for some people can remain calm and effective under a great deal of stress, while others fold up and become irrational under very little. Similarly, jobs make their different demands from this point of view. There is, however, a further point which concerns the kind of stress that crops up frequently. This is the stress of living among other people and particularly of working with them. Practical problems usually have an answer, and once this has been found, they remain answered. Problems involving people do not always have an answer, but have to be lived with. Moreover, when we think we have answered them in one way, they crop up again in another way. Thus the kind of part an individual can play successfully among others is largely determined by his emotional adjustment. We must therefore set out the demands of jobs from this point of view as objectively as we can.

The foregoing five headings serve to provide a framework which is reasonably comprehensive. When we are considering the specification of personal qualities required by a job, they can be set out in this manner. Scales can be set up under each heading based on a Normal Curve of Distribution (Fig. 3) so that we can use the average of the population as a reference point in our assessments.

Assessing the individual

Once the demands of the job, or the Personnel Specification, are complete we can be clear about the kind of person we are looking for. This leads on to the next question which is whether we can recognize him when we see him. How do the qualities we have set out in our Five-Fold Framework manifest themselves in a form that can be summed up in the course of an interview?

Our first heading, Impact on Others, presents few problems. Twenty minutes of conversation with someone should make it clear whether he

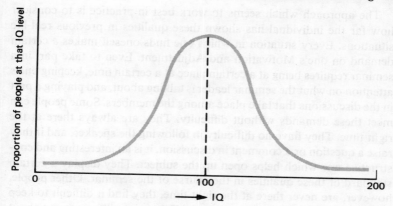

Fig. 3. If a quality has this sort of 'normal' distribution the average is clearly a useful and meaningful quantity, whereas if most people were either IQ 10 or IQ 190 the average would be of no real value at all since almost nobody would have it. It is suggested that by setting up a 'scale' for each of the five qualities (say 0 to 200!) and by using the mean as a reference point we can make meaningful comparisons between people in those qualities because we assume the qualities to be 'normally' distributed.

can express himself effectively and whether his manner is self-confident yet at the same time sufficiently sensitive to the reactions of others, while his dress and appearance can be summed up more or less at first glance. So long as we are reasonably sure about the standards on which we are judging, and so long as we are keeping this heading separate from the others, we should have no difficulty about making up our minds in the course of an interview.

Our second heading, Qualifications, is almost equally straightforward. Certificates, examinations, years of experience in different kinds of posts—these can be elicited without difficulty. They can even be obtained from an application form which will show at once whether or not it is worth while spending time on interviewing the candidate.

Brains or Abilities can be estimated by intelligence tests, and if it is considered worth the time and expense to apply these, a reasonably accurate assessment can be obtained.

It is in the remaining two headings, Motivation and Adjustment, that we are presented with our greatest difficulties of assessment, and as these are frequently the most important, we must spend a little time in deciding the kind of evidence that may be available on which to base a judgment.

The approach which seems to work best in practice is to consider how far the individual has shown these qualities in previous real-life situations. Every situation in which one finds oneself makes a certain demand on one's Motivation and Adjustment. Even to take part in a seminar requires being at a certain place at a certain time, keeping one's attention on what the seminar leader is talking about, and playing a part in the discussions that take place among the members. Some people can meet these demands without difficulty. They are always there at the right time. They have no difficulty in following the speaker, and if they raise a question or a comment in discussion, it is an interesting and constructive one which helps open up the subject. They display a certain standard of these qualities in the course of the seminar. Other people, however, are never there at the right time, they find it difficult to keep their attention on what is going on, and if there is a silly argument about nothing at all, they are in the middle of it! Such people show a different standard of Motivation and Adjustment in the same situation. Fundamentally, it is just as simple as that, for if we follow these people into different situations it very frequently happens that they display similar qualities wherever they go.

The evidence on which to base our assessment, therefore, lies in finding out about what an individual has made of the various situations in which he has found himself. The purpose of the interview is to obtain this information as fully as possible in the time available. And the most systematic way of doing this is to cover the whole life history. This will show how far he has met the demands of a number of situations and made use of the opportunities they have offered. Any life history can be sub-divided into the following stages.

Home background

It may seem odd to start off at the very beginning and find about where an individual's childhood was spent, but this is important in giving us the starting-point. Achievement can only be judged in terms of the starting-point, and if someone's father was a building labourer and he was the middle one of eight children, then he would have very few opportunities indeed handed to him on a plate. Compared with someone whose father was comfortably off and who could provide more guidance and opportunities, if the two had reached the same level in later life it would be obvious that the first had shown the greater motivation. Finding out about the home background can present its problems, for many people are self-conscious about their parents' situation in life.

Nevertheless, it is essential to know what opportunities were available to the individual originally if we are to decide how far he has come from his origins.

School

This is the first environment in which the young person finds himself on level terms with his contemporaries, and where his performance depends on the kind of qualities he shows. His record in examinations, which may depend on the kind of school, his part in games and other school activities, whether he was given office as a prefect or captain of a house—all these show how far his Motivation and Adjustment have been in action in the environment. So long as the interviewer is familiar with the various kinds of environment which different types of school present, he should not find it difficult to decide on how far they met their demands and made use of the opportunities they presented.

Further education

If the individual continues his education on a full-time basis at a university or college, this is simply another environment which has a considerable amount in common with school. The degree or qualification he has obtained, the part he has played in student games or activities, whether he was elected to office in any clubs or societies, whether he took an active part in student affairs—all these will be evidence of the kind of qualities he has manifested in this environment. It is important to remember, however, that it takes more Motivation and Adjustment to obtain the same qualification by part-time study, as this makes inroads on the individual's spare time and can conflict with other activities.

Working life

Each job is an environment which makes its own demands and offers its own opportunities. Thus if an individual appears to have been consistently offered additional responsibility at work, if he has stayed a reasonable time in his jobs, and if he has moved upwards from one to another, then we can be reasonably sure that the people with whom he has worked have found him an effective and responsible colleague. If, on the other hand, he has never stayed very long in one job, if he has never been entrusted with additional responsibility, and if the next job he has moved to was no better than the one before, then we can conclude that he has not shown the qualities we are interested in to any great extent in his working life. Some people's work history is a pattern of steadily increasing scope and responsibility, while others seem always to remain about the same level. Others again seem to slip gradually down the scale. In each of these cases it is pretty obvious what levels of Motivation and Adjustment they have demonstrated.

Service life

This is getting a little out of date now, but up till a few years ago most young men had a period in the Armed Forces. This presents another environment with its demands and opportunities.

Spare time

It may seem odd to want to know what an individual does in his leisure time, but, following the approach outlined above, this is simply another environment in which he can show the qualities we are looking for, or the lack of them. Moreover, in his spare time, a person has a wider liberty of choice in what he does. Thus the kind of activities he pursues, whether these involve initiative, as with playing games, do-it-yourself jobs and the like, or whether they are passive, like watching television or immersing oneself in a crowd of spectators at a football match or at a race meeting, are of interest in indicating the kind of personal qualities he is manifesting in this area of his life-pattern.

Present circumstances

Whether the individual is married or single, whether he has a family at school, whether he owns his house, these and other aspects of his present way of life may have some importance in summing him up. They may be particularly significant if we expect him to move to a different part of the country or even go abroad.

Once this amount of information has been accumulated about an individual it will usually be pretty clear what kind of personal qualities he is likely to manifest in a future situation. This method is known as Biographical Interviewing, and the rationale easily makes itself clear. Judgments are valid only when they are based on reliable evidence, and the above kind of evidence, when it has been patiently accumulated, provides the best guide to the individual's future performance. Some may be obtained by the use of an application form, but a well-conducted interview will always provide more evidence and make it easier to interpret this evidence than a mere outline. To be able to get this evidence in a twenty-minute interview, however, demands certain skills on the part of the interviewer.

Points for discussion

How essential are Job Descriptions?

Outline the Five-Fold Framework for Selection Interviewing.

What do we mean by a person's Adjustment?

What does Home Background indicate in regard to a person's achievements?

Discuss Biographical Interviewing.

9 Conducting the Interview

'Reason and judgment are the qualities of a leader'

Tacitus

The object of the interview is to obtain the information on which a valid assessment of the applicant may be based. We have already outlined the framework of the biography which contains this information, and the problem now becomes how to draw this out in the time available. This is basically a matter of encouraging the applicant to talk freely and frankly, and to get him to talk about what we want to hear.

Perhaps the most important point to make is that the interviewer must be able to subordinate his personality in the course of the interview. This is what many people find difficult or impossible, for they are so used to the idea that they are the 'big shot' in the interview situation. They ask the questions, they evaluate the answers, and they sit behind the desk and make the final decision. In such a situation the applicant is a lower order of life, waiting deferentially for the interviewer to make up his mind. It is difficult to imagine a situation less calculated to encourage the applicant to talk freely about himself, or to bring out the kind of information in which you are interested.

The interviewer must learn, therefore, that he must climb down from his 'big shot' position. He must build up the applicant's self-confidence by listening sympathetically and encouragingly to what he has to say. He must offer a continual series of responses which reassure the applicant that he is being taken seriously. The interviewer must fade into the background and become little more than an attentive and sympathetic listener. It is the applicant who should do most of the talking in the course of the interview. Similarly, the interviewer shows no surprise or criticism at anything the applicant tells him. If he gives any evidence of disapproval, then from that point onwards, the interview is slanted. The applicant will be careful to tell him only what he thinks he will approve of. He will be concealing or flanelling over anything that he thinks the interviewer will disapprove of.

One method of putting the point is to ask how much should the applicant remember about the interviewer after the interview is over. The answer is, very little. Simply that he seemed a reasonable chap who was most interested in everything the applicant told him. This is the criterion of how far the interviewer has succeeded in subordinating himself and handing the role over to the interviewee.

Contact or 'rapport' is the first and most essential factor in a successful interview. In some cases it can build up quickly and easily as the applicant finds that he is listened to sympathetically and encouraged to talk freely about himself. In other cases it may be more difficult, but a point to remember is that the most encouraging thing to an individual in this situation is the sound of his own voice. It may be necessary to go rather slowly at first in such cases and to let the applicant gain confidence gradually. As time goes on he will open up and the tempo will quicken.

Each interviewer will have his own individual style, and it is always a mistake to try to alter this to something which doesn't feel right. The same fundamental objective should be borne in mind, however, that it is the applicant who should do most of the talking and that you, the interviewer, should never try to impose yourself on the situation.

Content is the next point to be borne in mind. This concerns the amount of factual information which the interviewer is eliciting. We have already outlined what is required and after the interview it should be possible to recapitulate the life-history in detail. To do this effectively it will be necessary to take some notes, and this may involve a certain amount of practice if the 'contact' is not to suffer. A skilled interviewer should be able to scribble enough on a suitable form without interfering with the flow of the interview.

Control is the third aspect of the interview, and this means that it is going the way the interviewer wants in the time at his disposal. If the control is too obtrusive, however, 'contact' may be lost, and if this is lost it will be impossible to obtain 'content'.

One way of describing the interview is to think of two levels in the mind of the interviewer. The surface level is concerned with 'contact' and gives the impression that the interviewer has nothing else to do than listen to this fascinating story he is being told. At the back of his mind, he is checking up what information he is getting and thinking 'That sums up the home background, reasonably comfortable and encouraging. Now what about school? Yes, eight 'O' levels, three 'A' levels, that sounds all right. Games? Played for the first team at football and House Captain of cricket, that's fine. School offices? Prefect and vice-captain of the House. What else have we at school? Debating Society? Dramatic Society? Anything else? How's the time going? Fifteen minutes left so we'd better speed it up a bit'. This is the Content and

Control level of the interviewer's mind, and while it does not show on the surface, it is important if a complete case-history is to be obtained.

Sometimes the question is raised about whether you can rely on what you are told in the interview or whether you are getting a slanted or distorted story. This depends on the skill of the interviewer, for anyone can tell a lie. What is more difficult, however, is to make the second one fit with the first, and the third fit with the other two. As has already been said, a skilled interviewer never shows surprise or criticism. Thus the liar is encouraged to think that he is getting away with it. He will thus go on elaborating his fictitious story, and it will become increasingly obvious that the loose ends are not fitting together. A really skilled interviewer is a very difficult person to deceive, for while he appears to be taking it all in, he is in fact, weighing up and evaluating everything that he is being told. And any inconsistencies will very soon become noticeable.

Example of a biographical interview

Interviewer: Good Morning. Come in and sit down. It's Mr Jones, isn't it? Now, I've got you application form here so I know the outline of your background but I'd like to fill in a few more details. I see your address is Rockton. Have you always lived there?

Applicant: No. We moved there only five years ago when I got my present job.

I. And before that?

A. Up in Lancashire—just north of Manchester.

I. That's mainly textiles isn't it? Was your father in textiles?

A. Yes, he was a tackler.

I. That's a skilled job, isn't it?

A. Yes. Setting up the looms and dealing with any breakdowns. He was in it all his life but things began to change as he got older. He is retired now.

I. I see. Many in the family?

A. Three brothers and four sisters. I was one of the youngest.

I. That's quite a big family.

A. Yes. In these days it probably is. But when I was young it was pretty normal in the working areas.

I. Looking back on it now, what does it seem like?

A. It was almost a different world. My father had a steady job and mother looked after the house. There was no money, of course, but we all mucked in and helped. There was a certain security in spite of it all.

(*Interviewer notes:* working-class background with limited opportunities. Stable family, however, with no signs of emotional stress.)

I. Then, what about school?

A. I went to the local Primary School and then on to the Grammar School.

I. You passed the 'eleven-plus'?

A. Yes, I was lucky at that but I couldn't stay long. I had to leave at sixteen because father was on short-time.

I. Did you manage any 'O' levels?

A. Yes, I got six. English Language and Literature, Maths, Physics, Chemistry and Metal-work.

I. That was pretty good. How were you coming out in classes?

A. I was fairly well up. They wanted me to stay on for my 'A' levels but it just wasn't possible.

I. What about games?

A. I played for the school at football and was in the House team at cricket. I ran for the school in my last year.

I. You made good use of your opportunities then?

A. I think so. If I'd stayed on as they wanted me to, I might have gone a bit further, been a prefect and so on. But I had to start supporting myself.

(*Interviewer notes:* good achievement at school in relation to home background. Motivation and Adjustment well up).

I. So when you left school, what happened then?

A. I got a job as an apprentice with one of the local engineering companies. They gave me day-release at the local Technical College.

I. How did you get on there?

A. Not badly. I got my Ordinary National in Mechanical Engineering. Then I went on to Production Engineering and got my Higher National in that.

I. What made you change over?

A. Well, I didn't see much scope in the apprenticeship. It was mostly helping the tradesmen who were usually on maintenance, and there didn't seem much future in that sort of work. So I got moved into the Production Control Department.

I. What did you do there?

A. To begin with I wasn't much more than an office boy, but I gradually got on to helping with the production programmes. After a couple of years or so I was made a Progress Chaser in a small department. This meant I was responsible for seeing that the components came through on time and that the production programmes were being met.

I. How old were you then?

A. I'd have been about twenty-two or thereabouts. I'd finished my apprenticeship by then.

I. How did it go?

A. It nearly drove me round the bend at first, dealing with foremen who thought I was getting too big for my boots. But I managed to get them to co-operate eventually and it all settled down. We stepped up production a bit once I realized where the hold-ups were always cropping up.

I. So what happened then?

A. After a couple of years or so there was a vacancy in the Work Study Department. I applied for it and was moved in as a junior work-study officer and started off on rate-fixing. That was an awful job, with continual arguments with shop stewards and production workers. Up 'till then it had been old-fashioned piecework and management was trying to bring in more systematic work measurement. We made some progress, but it was difficult with all the old 'custom and practice' ideas and the tradition that everything had to be bargained over.

I. How long did you carry on?

A. For about three years.

I. Then you went to another job?

A. That's right. I began to feel that there wasn't much of a future for me. I was getting a bit more responsibility but it was going to take a long time to get the system working properly. Also, I could see that we weren't fitting in the production planning as we should have done. Ideally, we should have been able to lay out an exact programme based on work-measurement so that the plant could be kept working as near 100% capacity as we could manage. We never came within a mile of that, and I began to feel I was wasting my time. So when the next job was offered to me I decided to take it.

I. What was that?

A. Well, it was a small firm, employing less than a hundred. I'd met the owner's son at the Technical College and we got friendly. He was mainly interested in sales—they made various household gadgets—and he wasn't happy about their production side. So he introduced me to his father, and after we'd talked it over he offered me the job as factory manager.

I. That must have been a bit of a change.

A. Not really. You see, I'd always been in touch with the factory floor and I could see how so many management techniques went wrong when they got down there. So it was interesting to be in direct charge and to be able to follow things up on the job.

I. Did you set up a production control department?

A. Not really, the place wasn't big enough. I had a couple of clerks who worked out the orders and listed the components and raw materials. We drew up a sort of outline programme which I passed on to the foremen. The place was sub-divided into half a dozen sections, and it was not difficult to keep in touch with what was going on in each of them. If any hold-ups occurred we could switch things round a bit to keep them going. We usually managed to meet our delivery dates.

I. So it turned out successfully?

A. I think so. The owner and his son were quite pleased with the way the business built up and I believe the profit margins improved. We'd very little labour trouble, for in a small firm you've got advantages if you know how to make the most of them.

I. So why did you pack it in?

A. Well, after four years or so it was obvious that I'd got as far as I could go there. There was no chance of the firm expanding for they hadn't got the capital and I wasn't getting much of a salary. I was getting on for thirty and I was married with one child and another on the way. So I realized that if I wanted to get on in the world I'd have to make a move. I was sorry in a way for I liked the job and I got on well with the others, but when I thought it all out I decided that I'd have to find something else.

I. So that was when you moved to your present job? Tell me about that.

A. Well, as you know, Associated Components is a biggish company, with about five thousand employees. We're in light engineering, mainly machining and assembly work. I'm responsible for production planning and control, which means that I've got to see that orders are delivered on time on the one hand. On the other, I've got to make sure that our production facilities are kept fully occupied.

These are the two main targets of the job, and it's not always easy to achieve them both at the same time.

I. How do you think you've done?

A. Well, over the five years since I've been there we have made some progress. We've cut down the proportion of late deliveries and our output in relation to plant capacity has risen quite substantially. We keep figures for these things and they've been very satisfactory.

I. I suppose you have a fair number of staff under you.

A. Yes, We're sub-divided into five major departments and I've got an assistant production controller in charge of each. They have got their own programmers, progress chasers and work-measurement people. It adds up to between thirty and forty.

I. Tell me about the major problems you come up against.

A. Well, there are the deliveries on the one hand. Some of our customers have a rush order and we've got to let them have their components the day before yesterday! This means shifting around the production schedules and trying to get the materials through on time. That's run-of-the-mill stuff, of course, and we try to take it in our stride. What's rather more tricky is our relations with the production staff. If we're not careful we can get across the managers and supervisors because they think we're interfering with their responsibility. It's our job to sort out their programmes and it's their job to put them into effect. But there's always a bit of an overlap that needs some tactful handling and one can't always be sure that this will be forthcoming. I don't think we do too badly, but this is one of the problem areas. Then there are the shop stewards. They feel they should have a say in what's happening and if they think they're being overlooked or by-passed they can make a bit of trouble. But that's what you have to put up with and you can't afford to let it get you down.

I. Have you taken any further qualifications since you left the Technical College?

A. I'm a Member of the Institute of Production Engineers and the Institute of Work Study Practitioners. I've attended various short courses and conferences on different management subjects, but none of these has led to any actual qualifications.

(*Interviewer notes:* Further education up to professional standard by part-time study. Progress from apprenticeship to progress chaser, work-study department, then factory manager and finally production controller of present company. Seems to have been consistently successful in all these jobs and to have coped successfully with increasing responsibility. Motivation and Adjustment well up.)

I. So that brings us up to date. Is there anything we've missed?

A. I don't think so.

I. Now, outside of your work, how are you fixed?

A. I'm married, as you know, and we've got two children, a boy and a girl. He's getting on for seven so he's started school. She's a couple of years younger and she goes to a sort of nursery school for a bit in the morning.

I. Does your wife have a job?

A. Not a proper one. She helps out a bit at the local Old Peoples' Home, mainly in the office. She used to be a secretary. But with two young children she feels that they are her main responsibility just now.

I. Have you any hobbies?

A. Well, I do a bit around the house, painting and decorating, if you call that a hobby. Then there's the garden. We grow most of our own vegetables. I try to get a round of golf in on the week-ends to keep in shape but that's about all.

I. Reading?

A. I do quite a bit of reading. There are the journals from the various societies and I try to keep up with the reviews. I've written one or two articles that have been published.

I. That's rather interesting. They were on production control, I suppose?

A. Yes, about the kind of problems you come up against in batch production.

(*Interviewer notes:* Spare time mainly concerned with home and family but some initiative in his intellectual interests.)

    I. Good. Well, I think that covers your background adequately. Now I'd like to go into more detail about this post . . .

The interviewer then deals with matters relevant to the job under consideration, but by this stage he has enough information available to make a fair assessment of the applicant. By drawing him out in conversation he has given him the opportunity to show his self-confidence and ability to express himself. In this case he would obviously be given a high mark for Impact on Others. His Qualifications and Experience would also be clear by now and these appear to be up to management level. No test scores are available, but his qualifications suggest that he is reasonably high from this point of view.

In terms of Motivation it is obvious that wherever he has been he has made progress and has met the demands of his job satisfactorily. It is not without interest that his home background provided him with few opportunities but that he has been able to find these for himself. His pattern of consistent achievement in various situations makes it obvious that he is well up the scale from this point of view. The same impression is gained of his Emotional Adjustment, for he has coped successfully with responsibility and moved to jobs which made higher demands which he has met without difficulty.

The following few pages are devoted to points which the businessman unfamiliar with interviewing should bear in mind.

Purpose

When we have to deal with an interview we should approach it from two points of view. The first of these concerns its purpose, which is usually straightforward. The purpose of a selection interview is to collect the information on which an assessment can be based. The purpose of an exit interview is to uncover the real reasons why the individual is leaving the organization. The purpose of the grievance interview is to get the individual to open up and tell you what is on his mind.

Interaction

But over and above the purpose there is also the interaction between the people involved in the interview. This is a little more subtle, for it is not always entirely rational. The interaction can be affected by the kind of initiative which each one takes, how the other responds, the impressions they form of each other, their emotional reactions, and so on. If the interaction builds up in a positive manner it will facilitate the achievement of the interview's purpose. But if it works out negatively it will make the achievement of this purpose more difficult. It may even render it impossible, as when the interviewee bursts out with 'What the hell's that got to do with you? I didn't come here to be put through a Gestapo interrogation!' In such a case the interaction has broken down and the interview is a complete flop.

Social roles

Perhaps the simplest way to deal with this interaction is to think in terms of social roles. What kind of role is the interviewer taking? Is he firing quick questions and acting as the important person in the interview? If so, he is taking the dominant role and is forcing the interviewee into a subordinate one. Roles are interdependent, and each is the counterpart of the other. If we push the interviewee into an inferior role, is this likely to encourage him to talk freely and frankly? Or will it rather put him on the defensive, so that he clams up and responds as little as possible? If the interviewer thinks for a moment of the social role he wants the interviewee to take to him, he will quickly realize the kind of role he must take to the interviewee. If the purpose of the interview will be achieved only when the interviewee opens up and talks confidently, then the interviewer must adopt the role of an interested and sympathetic listener.

Curiously enough, it is the direct question which emphasizes the kind of role which the interviewer should try to avoid. For example:

Interviewer's question: What is your present job?
Interviewee's answer: I'm an assistant production manager with Brown and Robinson.
Q: How long have you been there?
A: Three years.
Q: Where were you before that?
A: With International Manipulators.
Q: How long were you with them?
A: Two years.

Starting off in this way puts the interviewee into the role of 'question answerer', deprives him of any initiative in the interaction and makes it pretty obvious that he is the inferior of the two. If the interview goes on like this he will feel more and more on the defensive and ill at ease. If, on the other hand, the interviewer can play down the importance of his position he may encourage the interviewee to adopt a more active role. For example:

Q: Now I'd like to find out a little more about your present job. Would you mind telling me something about it?
A: Well, I'm the assistant production manager in the assembly department.
Q: That involves production programming, I suppose?
A: Yes. It's a jobbing department and we've got to make sure the

components are ready on time.
Q: Otherwise you get hold-ups?
A: Yes. It's sometimes a bit of a problem keeping everything going. We can't always rely on deliveries from the suppliers and things can go wrong in the machine shop. So we've got to switch things round to keep the men occupied, and that's not always very popular. Then there's our own deliveries. Customers don't like to be kept waiting.
Q: Yes, I can see that. Tell me a bit more about the department.
A: Well, we've got about fifty assemblers, mostly semi-skilled . . .'

In this situation the interviewee has found himself talking to an interested and sympathetic listener which is the role which the interviewer intended to adopt. As a result he has felt quickly at ease, has opened up and talked with increasing freedom. The role he has been offered in the interview has built up his self-confidence and he has found it easy to express himself in it. This is what the interviewer intended, and by taking his 'interested listener' role he has encouraged the interviewee to adopt its counterpart.

Even though he avoids the direct question for the most part in a selection interview, the interviewer can lead the applicant through his present and previous jobs, his school and further education. Prompts and leads like 'And after that, I suppose, you decided to . . .', 'That would get you involved in organizing . . .' will encourage the interviewee to open up and go into detail about what he has done. The ground can thus be covered, and he is unobtrusively guided through the biography by his interviewer. One point which should be emphasized is his responses. Whatever the interviewee says should be met with a gesture of appreciation. These may be verbal like 'That's very interesting. Tell me a bit more about it'. Or they may be non-verbal in the form of nods or interested gestures. If no such responses are forthcoming and the interviewee feels that he is talking to a blank wall he will very quickly dry up. If, on the other hand, he feels that the interviewer is taking in everything he says and responding positively to it, he will find it satisfying to talk to him and will express himself more freely.

There are, of course, two halves to a selection interview. One is aimed at finding out about the applicant, and we hope that a serviceable method for this has been outlined. The other is concerned with letting the applicant find out about the job, for no one should start in a post without knowing exactly what is required of him, the conditions of employment and the opportunities it offers. Provided that a suitable interaction has been built up it should not be difficult for the interviewer to switch from one to the other. He might say:

Interviewer: Well, I think we've covered your background adequately so we can now turn to the job and the organization. You've already seen something about it in the advertisement but I expect you want a good deal more detail. Where would you like me to begin?

Interviewee: Could you tell me a bit more about the department I'd be responsible for and whom I'd be responsible to?

Interviewer: Certainly. It's a production department employing a hundred and fifty men. The equipment is semi-automated . . .'

Closing an interview

The ideal appointment should offer the individual scope for his abilities and a satisfying sense of achievement. It should also provide the organization with an individual whose performance contributes to its efficient operation. Thus if the interviewer can close the interview by saying 'Now, do you think this is the kind of job you're looking for?' and the interviewee can reply 'Yes, I think it's the job for me', then the two have apparently been reconciled. To imagine that this will work out every time is perhaps rather starry-eyed, but it should be borne in mind as the result of a successful selection interview.

In some cases it may be possible to close the interview by offering the applicant the job. Usually, however, there will be other applicants to see, so that an immediate decision cannot be announced. The interviewee should then be told that a letter will be sent informing him of the decision and this should be got off with the minimum of delay. There is nothing more irritating than having to hang on while an employer makes up his mind. One point that might be mentioned is that a negative decision should always be sent by letter. Telling an applicant that he is not suitable for a job usually leads him to ask where he falls short. If the interviewer then tries to explain that his experience is not exactly what the company are looking for, the applicant will argue that they haven't realized that in one of his previous jobs his experience was extremely relevant. This may lead the interviewer to point out other shortcomings so that the way is open to bad-tempered argument which does neither side any good. The image of the employing organization may suffer, and in a tight labour market it is important to preserve a reputation of being a good employer.

Points for discussion

What is the object of a selection interview?

The three essentials of an effective interview have been defined as contact, content and control. How would you interpret these factors in a selection interview? (AIA)

How should an interviewer subordinate his personality in the course of an interview?

Where does the concept of 'social roles' fit into interviewing?

What are your recommendations in regard to the closure of the interview?

What points would you include in a check-list for those who wish to improve their performance as interviewers? (AIA)

10 Communicating with Employees

'It is reason and speech that unite men to one another; there is nothing else in which we differ so entirely from the brute creation'

Cicero

It's a spartan existence on America's last frontier, where the Alyeska Pipeline Service Company is laying the trans-Alaskan pipeline, the most expensive construction project in history. They work up to twelve hours a day, seven days a week, in which temperatures can fall to 55 below freezing! There are few women—no liquor. The only contact with the outside world is by radio telephone.

But the workers are kept sweet and hard working by big money—around $2,000 a month, and by (for construction workers) lush camp conditions such as carpeted, well-furnished rooms, well-stocked libraries and daily movies.

Cash is a crude but powerful method of communicating with the workers when the job is especially tough. One reason is the symbolic significance of money. During the national mineworkers' strike in the UK in 1972 one union leader said: 'Our men spend all day in dangerous, unhealthy jobs, yet their daughters, working as secretaries, earn as much as they do.' How much pay-turmoil is really about recognition and self respect—both much harder to give than money.

Subtler methods needed

Workers in many factories find it difficult to feel much self-respect: 'You'd treat a dog better than this, give it a longer leash', a car worker complained. 'A man's work station is the length of the car body plus three feet either end and he has to stay in it'. In some plants a man can't even go to the lavatory until the spare man arrives to take his place on the track.

'When I'm here my mind's a blank. I make it go a blank.' It takes more than incentives to cut through cynicism as deep as this. Subtler communication techniques are needed.

I've heard of bakery workers who were so turned-off with their jobs

69

that they simply walked out in mid-shift and didn't even come back for their wages.

Walter Reuther, the American union boss, in describing the plight of many industrial workers, evoked a Chaplinesque vision of men crushed in the cogs: 'The prospect of tightening bolts every ten minutes for eight hours a day for thirty years doesn't exactly lift the human spirit.'

The facts of industrial life can cause a tremendous build-up of frustration and resentment which vents itself in poor work, absenteeism, hostility to management—even outright violence. In *Working for Ford* Hugh Benyon reports bostic bombs being hurled by frustrated workers into rubbish dumps at one of Ford's UK plants.

Turned-off workers

How many bruising confrontations in industry stem from these pent-up frustrations? At a Liverpool factory in 1975 management and workers locked horns over the vital issue of where the wages should be handed out. The workers felt so 'bolshy' that they refused to allow management into the factory to distribute them there. Management retaliated by stopping workers going into the office block and collecting them there. A compromise was worked out. The wages were handed out through a side-window while workers queued in the rain.

How can you communicate with your work force in spite of the frustrations and aggressions that may exist? One hundred and thirty years ago, Disraeli wrote about 'two nations ... as ignorant of each other's habits, thoughts and feelings as if they were dwellers in different zones or inhabitants of different planets'. Today a cleavage in social ethics still exists, and it separates the manager from his work force—unless he knows how to bridge the gap.

Close co-operation between the two sides of industry during the three-day week period in 1974 shows that genuine communication can take place. But too many managers still regard industrial relations as somebody else's business. Hugh Parker, head of McKinsey's consultancy operation in the UK points out that 'people who manage don't identify themselves with the interests of the managed. They stay aloof—at arm's length from the workers'. Here are some techniques for getting closer to your work force.

Group sessions

Many companies, such as the Japanese giant, Matsushita, find that the group session attended once a week, say, by the entire staff of a section or department or division is an effective communication method.

The meetings should be as informal as possible so that everyone is encouraged to talk. In a relaxed atmosphere management can explain its plans and policies and tell the employees what is happening to the goods they are producing—remind them of their important contribution.

Work can be freely discussed, improvements suggested, and the workers can buttonhole their bosses and air their grievances. Policies can be explained. The advantage of doing it this way is that once the whole group accepts the need for a change of plan or procedure, individuals who are hostile to management tend to adjust to the new conformity. Some men take pride in defying management but think twice before opposing their own work mates.

Informal meetings with workers' representatives

An engineering firm's management which in previous years had met union officials only at times of crisis decided to ask the union to meet them regularly, reason or no reason. So, once a week the two sides met—just sat and talked informally. For the first time each side found itself really listening and being interested in the other. Each side was able to explain its own point of view and, because of the informal atmosphere, really wanted to learn the other side's view.

Each meeting brought a quick exchange of pieces that brought both sides closer to their common objective—compromise, and therefore stability across the industrial board.

When the number of disputes in the factory dropped, management linked the trend with these informal meetings. Thus they soon paid for themselves many times over.

When people from the two sides of industry sit informally round the same table they begin to understand one another's viewpoint. When they sit round the table long enough and often enough they even begin to share the same values and talk the same language.

Of course the communication barriers will remain unless the unions feel that management are really listening during these meetings and will take action as a result of what they hear.

More contact with union leaders

Many unions are better at fighting management than at co-operating with it to achieve joint goals. One clue in dealing with awkward union branches comes from F. M. Thrasher's book *Gang* based on his work with delinquent teenage gangs. He found that the best way to influence these gangs was through their leaders. By concentrating attention on the leader and showing him ways of achieving status and security—the main motives for gang membership—by other means than the gang, Thrasher was able to change the attitude of the whole gang. The rest followed the leader's example.

Perhaps, after all, the best way to deal with the militant shop steward or wildcat leader is not to isolate him, not to seek less contact but to seek more contact with him. Bring him onto the works committees. Give him special responsibilities—and therefore status. Ask him to chair staff meetings or group sessions. In this way you will involve the man and his followers in management processes.

Or carry involvement a stage further. Ask the local union branch to advise management about discipline and conditions of work—the length and times of tea-breaks, holiday and overtime arrangements and so on. This kind of direct involvement in management creates a greater sense of responsibility in union members, a greater awareness of management problems.

Supervisory interviews

Supervisory interviews, held about twice a year, can raise morale and improve communication between employee and first-line management. Supervisors who are trained to conduct these interviews should be fully briefed about aims and techniques to ensure (a very difficult task) that employees will feel free to talk without inhibition.

During the interview, the employee is given an appraisal of his performance over the past half-year together with advice about how to improve. We need to remember that many workers lose heart because they genuinely don't know how they are measuring up to company expectations: nobody ever tells them.

Then it is the employee's turn to talk about his or her problems and grievances, or about anything else they want to get off their chests.

Western Electric has found that supervisors who are involved in these interviews become less dogmatic in their ideas, more willing to take account of the feelings of their subordinates. The first-line manager is brought into closer contact with his people, perhaps in spite of himself.

Success depends largely on the social skills of the interviewer, his ability to establish an easy relationship with the other person. Thus the provision of effective company training in this field is essential. Chances of success are improved when:

(a)   the supervisor holds the interview on neutral ground and not in his own office;

(b)   is careful not to show too much authority;

(c)   encourages the employee (by using appropriate counselling techniques) to speak his mind;

(d)   does not argue, disagree, express shock or disapproval.

The value of technique

Areas like these show clearly that communication is above all a technique when applied to industry.

The inevitable social and environmental stresses which crop up in the industrial organization do not admit social contact between individual managers and employees in an entirely normal way. For the factory or the office is always an artificial environment in which individuals cannot choose each other's company.

The problem is compounded because of the frustrations and resentments that build up in the work force as a result of tedium and discipline. Such feelings are not dissolved by cash incentives, unless they are abnormally high.

In large organizations, formal patterns of communication will always predominate. But the trick is to promote better relations by encouraging informal communication between managers and employees.

This is not something that can happen overnight with some magic gesture. It will be the product only of a consistent management policy that sets out to win and deserve the confidence of the work force. To achieve that, management must not only accept the principle of good communication, but get down to the planning of a detailed campaign.

Such a campaign might be spearheaded by the techniques described above. But in any case, it will require the co-operation of the other side as a starting point.

Points for discussion

Discuss the 'symbolic significance of money'.

There are, unfortunately, various barriers to effective communication. Two of these are background and attitude. Describe what is meant by these terms in the context of good communication. (AIA)

What is the principal value of group sessions?

What are the likely advantages to a manager in having more contact with trade union leaders?

Discuss the supervisory interview.

'What matters at an interview is not what is said, but how it is heard'. How far do you think this is true? (ICSA)

11 In-company Communication Barriers

'Men are never so likely to settle a question rightly as when they discuss it freely'

Macaulay

Managers and workers have generally been to different schools. They live in different parts of town, go to different pubs, rarely mix socially. Neither learns the other's point of view. How many communication breakdowns in industry spring from this underlying experience gap? Perhaps nationwide comprehensive education would be a good long-term method of improving industrial relations in Britain!

No wonder that so many management announcements, filled with words like efficiency, productivity and profitability, fall on deaf ears: for managers are committed to these values whereas the workers' main aims at work are security and stable social relationships. Workers are group-minded whereas managers tend to be individualists striving for personal achievement and reward. To the manager, cash incentives seem the logical way to boost production. But the worker knows that striving for money might cut him off from his work-mates. How many bonus schemes have collapsed under the weight of this simple fact?

The manager needs to be aware of the cleavage in social ethics that separates him from his employees, and desist from making individualistic appeals to employees in trying to boost their production or improve their time-keeping.

Consider the problem of output restriction. To the worker this is a completely logical way of protecting himself against unreasonable demands or possible redundancies. Any attempt by management to convince individuals to the contrary will be fiercely resisted. Operatives will change their methods and raise their output only when the work group as a whole nods approval. To break through barriers of this kind, call the group together and explain why a change is necessary; offer new forms of security for old, e.g., guarantee jobs and earnings; then leave them to *talk themselves* into a change of attitude. Only in this way can the emotional barriers be overcome. Of course, such an approach carries risks: the discussion may lead to a hardening of attitudes rather than a change of heart.

But sometimes the employees should be encouraged to make their own decisions. An experiment was carried out in a toy factory where girls had complained about the speed of a moving belt carrying components for assembly. After discussions a control dial was fitted to the work bench so that the girls themselves could control the speed of the belt. The girls were very pleased and morale soared. And the average speed at which the girls themselves ran the belt was higher than the speed they had complained about!

Through participation management can increase its control by seeming to relinquish it. Furthermore, employees happily implement changes which they have decided upon or agreed to. And that is a valuable effect, for change itself is the only constant in modern industry.

Participating

Henry Ford was touring a new automated engine factory with Walter Reuther, President of the Auto Workers' Union. When Ford remarked to Reuther, 'Walter, these machines never go on strike', Reuther replied, 'True but they don't buy any automobiles either'. If you think about it Reuther's reply contains a sufficient reason for treating workers and their representatives with a special kind of courtesy and respect—the kind that would have seemed soft-headed a generation ago. One Managing Director at a motor components factory wouldn't agree with that proposition. When the union official called to talk about the case of a dismissed foreman the Managing Director sent a curt message saying he was too busy to see him. Next day the official made four 'phone calls only to be told each time that the MD was not available. So every foreman in the factory came out on strike in protest. Moral: avoid high-handedness—it doesn't pay.

Times have changed and workers have changed. Employees are better educated and more sophisticated than they were a few decades ago. The development of automation and electronics has caused a shift from craft skills to numerical control, with a consequent blurring of white and blue-collar distinctions. Employees are better equipped than they used to be to contribute to company plans and policies. Lord Feather, the former Secretary of the TUC, has said he'd like to see workers discussing such matters as manpower requirements, delivery dates, new machinery and other topics still widely considered to be the exclusive prerogative of management.

Many managers still jib at the thought of introducing wide-ranging consultative processes, fearing that to do so would be to relinquish some of their powers. Perhaps they are right. Perhaps each extra piece of participation machinery represents a real transfer of authority. But perhaps too the most formidable communication barriers in British industry can only be overcome by this kind of radical transformation.

A powerful braking-force on the trend towards decision-sharing is the undemocratic nature of most companies in Britain. The votes that control them go to money not people; the running is done by a small and powerful group of directors; power rests at the apex. No doubt within the next few years company law will be reformed to bring the voice of the work force in greater measure into the boardrooms. Such a reform is long overdue, for there are many areas where the experience of the man on the job can do much to improve methods and efficiency. As Mary Parker Follett pointed out half a century ago, the man who works with the machine is as expert about it in his way as the man who designs or the man who buys it. This is the assumption at Parish Instruments of Richmond, Surrey, where informal meetings were held on the factory floor during protracted tea breaks: company plans and problems are openly discussed with the Managing Director joining in.

At Rowan Engineering of Glasgow the staff decide most matters in the company, right down to electing managers and fixing their salaries. Matters of policy are decided by all employees. This approach has relieved the company of many financial problems. At Scott Bader job applicants are interviewed by some of the people they will be working over. While in the Computer Management group all levels have identical desks, the same carpet and the same amount of space. The Managing Director, in the middle of a large open-spaced office, may be freely approached at any time by anybody. As a result of this free communication many problem areas have been revealed and ironed out. One of the company's founders said 'We are like an army with only officers—the computer is our only private soldier'.

Talk to the union leaders

Through his union the worker has more direct influence over the conditions of his everyday life than he exercises by his vote at a General Election. But many managers see only the negative side of union activity, although the positive side is far more important. Think of how joint consultation in the coal mines enabled the smooth introduction of full mechanization and the planned closure of five hundred pits during Lord

Robens' time. Sir William Swallow has attributed his success in avoiding serious strikes at Vauxhall while he was at its head to the habit of constant discussions with the unions, so that grievances could be spotted as soon as they arose and acted on 'in minutes or hours'.

Talk to the workers' representatives and take them into your confidence: for they are a valuable communication channel for conveying information and feelings upwards and downwards, and for explaining management's plans and policies to the work force. The modern union boss talks about wages and prices in terms indistinguishable from those used by the CBI. Management and the unions are partners in industry if only they would acknowledge the fact.

Professor Tom Lupton of the Manchester Business School has shown that even the disruptive side of union activity may serve a positive purpose. The entire trade union machinery of strikes, ballot, go-slows, etc., acts as a kind of battering ram, smashing down barriers, forcing management to listen and to make necessary changes, clearing the ground for realistic policies.

Why upward communication gets blocked

Good upward communication gives management the information it needs for sound decision-making. It brings employees' on-line experience to bear on company problems, and acts as a kind of early-warning system about shop-floor problems and grievances. Yet in many firms upward communication works in low gear. Often the cause is a lack of listening ability in managers combined with over-reliance on formal channels for feeding information upwards. The inability to listen at top levels strangles the desire to tell at lower levels. According to M. H. Knowles, an industrial psychologist, many managers are constitutionally incapable of listening to subordinates. According to Knowles, it is the neurotic, authoritarian personality who tends to get himself promoted into a managerial position. Such people are incapable of expressing their own feelings or of listening properly to others.

But sometimes employees themselves are to blame for poor upward communication. Most of us tell the boss only what we think will please him, feeling we can't afford to expose our failures and weaknesses. In a study of fifty-two managers, Read found that men on the way up tend to restrict information about their problems because they want to please the boss and preserve comfortable work routines. The inevitable results of this kind of self-imposed censorship is that bugs in the system multiply. The 'ever open door' might as well be slammed shut if the men on either side of it won't talk frankly to each other.

There is much that the individual executive can do to stimulate upward communication with his own department or unit. For instance, he can seek personal contact with employees and attempt to learn their point of view, their goals and values. Other possible actions include:

(a) holding regular meeting with employees to discuss their problems and grievances;

(b) finding out which communication methods are preferred by employees and using them, e.g., the shop steward may be preferred by employees as a channel of upward communication;

(c) regularly checking that foremen are passing upwards information, ideas, grievances received from the shop floor.

This kind of systematic communication eats up time. But far more time can be spent ironing out the misunderstandings and grievances that arise when upward communication is neglected.

Why not use some of the following administrative techniques for stimulating upward communication in your own organization?

Set up a special section to collect information about employee attitudes and grievances. The information could be collected by anonymous questionnaires or by confidential interviews which are then sent to top management for use in policy making.

Confidential exit interviews would help you to discover workers' real reasons for leaving and perhaps several serious shortcomings in the company will be revealed.

Using an employee counsellor can have the double effect of boosting morale on the shop floor and revealing grievances before they become storm centres.

Informal get-togethers over coffee can greatly stimulate upward communication within the management team.

Polaroid Corporation employees can telephone a special number and state their grievances or question. Answers are sent direct to the employee and then printed in the company newspaper. Other companies fix certain times when top executives are available for 'phone calls from employees on any topic.

Suggestion schemes

Most employees have their own special work methods. They find short cuts. They develop quicker and easier ways of doing their jobs, like the machinist who raised his output by making a short rod for guiding a cutting tool. By tapping this kind of know-how, suggestion schemes not only reduce operating and production costs but also increase employee participation in company affairs.

Suggestion schemes act as a powerful stimulant to upward communication. That is why the Industrial Welfare Society has been supporting them since 1918. Today they operate in thousands of companies—sometimes with great success. One manager reports that a new company suggestion scheme paid for itself in the first week, because valuable ideas for cutting waste and rationalizing the work-flow were among the first to be contributed. Westinghouse Corporation reckons that in one year it saved more than a million and a half dollars through implementing suggestions. Yet it paid only a fifth of that amount back in awards.

Generous cash awards for accepted suggestions are an essential component of any scheme. As some companies have discovered, a tight-fisted policy by the suggestion committee can kill interest in the scheme and damage morale. Cash keeps the ideas flowing. Hundreds of money-making ideas for boosting productivity were dropped in the BLMC suggestion boxes after the company offered a new Mini car every month for the best suggestion. Many firms even pay for good rejected ideas as an acknowledgment of time and effort spent and as an encouragement to employees to keep trying. Some firms reward the section or department as well as the individual for an accepted suggestion and claim that this is a good way of raising morale throughout the plant.

In most companies suggestion schemes are used exclusively for ideas about technical improvements. But why not widen the scope of a company's suggestion scheme by inviting suggestions about company plans, policy and managerial methods then relaying all these suggestions direct to the Board.

Operating a suggestion scheme

A simple and easy way of operating a suggestion scheme is to invite employees to write out their ideas and drop them into boxes scattered throughout the factory. At weekly or fortnightly intervals, suggestions are collected and appraised either by assigned experts or by a Suggestions Committee—usually composed of managers and workers' representatives. Typically, about one suggestion in four is accepted, with full reasons being given for turning the other suggestions down. Accepted suggestions are then sent to top management who estimate the likely savings and fix the sizes of the awards. In most cases the award is between 10% and 20% of estimated savings in the first year.

An alternative method is to instruct each department to organize its own suggestion scheme and to submit the best ideas to top management for a final decision.

To maintain interest in the scheme, year after year, continuous publicity is essential. Try to deal with all suggestions quickly and thoroughly, and implement suggestions as soon after acceptance as possible, for nothing kills interest faster than tardiness and delay. Use the company suggestion scheme as an employee motivator by making sure that employees throughout the plant share in any savings. This could be done by raising the general bonus from time to time.

There is no reason why a suggestion scheme should rely entirely on written communication, so why not invite contributors to talk over their ideas with the suggestion committee? Often, as an idea is discussed and developed, it turns from good to excellent. And even if the idea is finally rejected it is easier, and better for the morale, to give the reasons in an informal discussion than by means of a formal letter.

In-fighting

Anyone who has worked in a large organization has experienced the aggressions, tensions and anxieties that infiltrate every office and workshop. Seen from this angle, the organization is a battlefield, where individuals and cliques emerge and fight each other for status and power and where the knives may be out waiting for the backs to turn! Fierce in-fighting erupts in every nook and cranny. Perhaps conflict of this kind is unavoidable—even a biological principle. Human nature is always there. The ancestral hunting-pack, but now in grey flannel suits.

The relevance of this to the communicator is that as messages fly to and fro across the battlefield they get torn and distorted. A dislikes B, so he sends a deliberately misleading message or says only what must be said and not one word more. B distrusts A, so he reads into his message all sorts of hidden threats and twisted motives.

In many companies the left hand never knows what the right hand is doing. It probably doesn't know what the left hand is doing either! How well do people understand their own emotions?

A way of opening people's eyes to their own blindness is to arrange a sensitivity-training course. Managers from different units are assembled and split into two groups. Each group presents a case to the other requesting some action—the release of certain statistics, let's say. Each group discusses the other's request. The discussions are taped and the tapes played back and analysed in terms of the amount of heat generated. Each side then describes how it viewed the other's motives—how it misinterpreted and misconceived—and describes the emotions it felt. Gradually the participants become aware of their own distorting aggressions and fears which affect the way they see and communicate with others in the organization.

You read with your feelings

People don't perceive the real thing. Facts become festooned with fantasy. In one experiment boys had to estimate the sizes of piles of coins. The greater the value of the coins the greater their overestimate of the size of the piles. They did not, however, overestimate the size of a pile of coin-shaped pieces of cork. The tendency to overestimate was greater in the poorer children.

Feelings can shrink a message. Karen Hornby, a psychiatrist, has observed how anxious people who feel under a threat actually observe less than when they are not feeling threatened. A man who is afraid of being made redundant may miss the point or not register part of your argument if you send him a reassuring memo.

Feelings can play tricks on your memory so that you vividly remember parts of the message but completely forget the rest. Rapoport reviewed experiments showing that pleasant material is remembered longer than unpleasant material. Agnes A. Sharp showed, in the *Journal of Experimental Psychology*, that acceptable phrases such as 'securing justice' were remembered longer than unacceptable phrases such as 'fearing poison'. The Rorschach ink-blot tests show that people project their own schemata onto what they see and hear. Into every message they read their own romance. Thus the same simple message changes its meaning as it passes from hand to hand for it can only have such meaning as the recipient's experience permits him to read into it.

An incomplete or poorly-worded message in particular invites people to use their own imagination to work it out. Consider this simple memo: 'After stopping the machine please check that safety guards are secure'. To one man this may mean 'I've been noticing how carelessly you operate the machine'. To another it may mean 'Don't knock off work early again, or you'll be sorry', and to a third 'I know I can rely on you to do the right thing'. To reduce the chances of your message being twisted in this way, why not pause for a moment before sending the message out; try to anticipate the possible ways in which the message might be misinterpreted so that you can make a point of stating that's not the meaning that should be read into it.

Group pressure can distort judgment. Asch studied college students' judgment of different professions. When told the other 500 students rated politics highest the subject tended to raise his own evaluation of the profession. In another famous experiment, 123 subjects were asked to say which of three lines was the same length as a standard line after five stooges had unanimously given a wrong judgment. 37% were wrong compared with 1% normally.

These are just some of the factors which conspire to twist even the simplest message as it passes up or down the line. In a large firm where there may be seven or eight levels between the Managing Director and the shop floor, a message can undergo a complete shift of meaning as it is relayed downwards.

Translating messages

Within a department communication may consist largely of technical information flowing between like-minded people. In such a case communication can be rich and accurate because similar training and experience have left these specialists with similar terms of reference. But when messages are sent *across* departments and levels they may become distorted.

This happens because people interpret messages and react to them in different ways according to their positions in the organization. You can never assume that your own vocabulary and values and expectations are the same as those of the people in the next office. Sending a message in the same basic English to all recipients is not good communication if everybody who reads it interprets it differently.

To reduce the chances of multiple interpretation you may need to 'translate' your message into several different 'languages' so that each group will understand it and respond to it in the way you intend. You may need to use several small communication loops instead of a single all-embracing loop. Stilletos rather than the club!

Suppose that you have to communicate details of a new holiday arrangement to everybody in the department. At first you think of pinning up a notice on the notice board for all to see—a single large communication loop. Then you remember that the last time you did this some of the supervisors complained about not being informed in advance of the general announcement. You also recall that some of the immigrant cleaners recently complained about not being able to understand the difficult language of many notice board announcements. So you decide to use a number of small communication loops and send several memos:

(1) *A memo for supervisors* to be handed to each man personally several days in advance of the general announcement. Full reasons for the change to be given.

(2) *A memo for operatives* to be posted on the central notice board a few days later and giving brief reasons for the change.

(3) *A memo for the cleaners* to be pinned up in the cleaners' tea room and written in very plain language, and explaining very simply what action must be taken and who to go to for further information.

Down go three potential communication barriers! And this approach also solves the problem of correct timing, i.e., making sure that people receive the message at the required time and in the right sequence.

Barriers caused by size and complexity

In most large organizations there are numerous communication gaps—between departments, between managers and workers, between experts in different disciplines, and so on. In large organizations especially, patterns of communication are complex and blockages or distortions can occur at numerous junctures. *Physical* distance between units and *Psychological* distance between specialists and different levels cause numerous communication breakdowns. H. Wilensky in his book *Organizational Intelligence* says:

> Even if the initial message is accurate, clear, timely and relevant, it may be translated, condensed or completely blocked by personnel standing between the sender and the intended receiver; it may get through in distorted form. If the receiver is in a position to use the message he may screen it out because it does not fit his preconceptions, because it has come through a suspicious or poorly regarded channel . . . or simply because too many messages are transmitted to him (information overload).

Moreover, as the number of experts proliferates so the jargon problem grows, with the walled-in specialist writing reports that only he can understand.

Hierarchy causes the strangling of upward communication; and centralization severs local experts and managers from decision-makers, which often leads to poor quality decisions. Communication failure is, in a sense, built into large and complex organizations. Hierarchy, centralization and specialization are essential—there would be no coordination or control without them. Yet their existence rules out a full and free information flow. Harold Wilensky has referred to some of the possible remedial actions: if a hierarchy is tall, flatten it; give more experts more autonomy by having them report to fewer bosses; set up interdepartmental task forces to break through the barriers separating departments; use secrecy only where functionally necessary.

The more complex the organization the more detailed are the steps management must take to ensure that information reaches all its parts and that information from all parts penetrates to the centre. A useful tactic to adopt within your own area of command might be to rationalize the work-flow so that fewer people are handling any particular piece of administration or production. Another useful reform might be to reduce the number of supervisory levels within the department or unit, so reducing the number of relay points at which the message can get blocked or twisted. Remember that the fewer people between sender and receiver the more accurate the message. Where possible, go direct.

Communication barriers topple when managers update their attitudes and start involving their employees in the management process. For instance, many large companies have overcome restriction of output and other industrial ailments by encouraging participation and decision-sharing. Remember how the Coal Board's habit of full consultation with the unions enabled planned closure of hundreds of pits. Some firms have improved efficiency and raised morale by inviting workers' representatives into boardrooms and listening to their ideas. Listening to the worker's voice gives management the information they need for sound decision making.

This kind of open-minded approach is doubly valuable when combined with an awareness of the emotional and group pressures that can twist even the simplest message, and a knowledge of the techniques for avoiding this kind of distortion. For instance, translating the same message into several different 'languages' so that each recipient understands it and responds to it in the way you intend. Perhaps, after all, the most formidable communication barriers can only be overcome by the kind of radical transformation in management thinking that this approach requires.

Points for discussion

Mention some of the communication barriers which commonly exist between managers and operatives and suggest how these barriers can be overcome. (AIA)

Why do upward communications get blocked?

What are the main advantages of a company's suggestion scheme?

In what circumstances would you translate the message you are sending to company employees?

Comment on the statement that 'hierarchy causes the strangling of upward communications'.

Give two main aims of a firm's suggestion scheme. Give the main points you would incorporate in a scheme you were asked to devise. (ICSA)

'Communication within a company can usually be improved so long as there is a genuine desire on the part of all concerned to bring about an improvement'. Comment on the matters which should receive attention in attempting to improve communication within an organization. (AIA)

What are the main channels of communication that can be used in a large organization to give information to employees? (ICSA)

12 Written Communication and Graphic Communication

'Hereafter, when trains moving in an opposite direction are approaching each other on separate lines, guards and drivers will be required to bring their separate trains to a dead halt before the point of meeting, and be very careful not to proceed until each train has passed the other'

From the Rule Book of the Cornwall Railway. c. 1873

Writing style

The first rule for good style is to have something to say; in fact, this in itself is almost enough. Business English is at most times clumsy and wordy, which constitutes not only an enormous waste of time and risk of confusion but also contributes very badly to a good commercial image. The great mathematician George Polya had this to say about style: 'The first rule of style is to have something to say. The second rule of style is to control yourself when, by chance, you have two things to say; say first one, then the other, not both at the same time.'

The reduction of communication to *writing* was a fundamental step in the evolution of society, for, besides being useful in situations where speech is not possible, writing permits the preservation of communications, or records, from the past. Indeed it is said that William Caxton made history, as far as writing is concerned, when he invented a foolproof method by which he could let his reader know when he had finished one thought and was about to begin another. That invention was the 'full stop' or 'period'. But the longer Mother Earth exists the more complicated she becomes, and before we look at style and coherence in greater detail let's just see the great number of written communications the average administrator originates or receives:

(1) Memoranda
(2) Letters
(3) Informal handwritten notes
(4) Minutes

86

(5) Reports
(6) Forms and Questionnaires
(7) Instructions
(8) Handbooks
(9) Manuals
(10) Documents

In any form of written communication there are three essentials to good style: (a) unity, (b) coherence, and (c) power.

The principle of unity applies on three levels: (1) the individual sentences must be unified; (2) individual paragraphs must be unified; and, naturally (3) the message as a whole must be unified.

The individual sentence must be *unified* in that it must convey only one main idea. Modifying ideas may be attached but the main idea must be all important. You must be direct, simple, brief, clear, and vigorous. Successful writing has a generous mixture of simple direct sentences. Flesch has this to say about sentences: 'When we try to imitate dialogue or conversation on paper, we naturally stick to short sentences and our average may run to fifteen or even ten words per sentence. But as soon as we get the itch to appear more serious and dignified, up it goes and we get more and more Victorian; and when we yield to the temptation of pompousness, we get downright monstrous and write sentences no man has ever said aloud.' Sentences in all good writing should generally be kept short. But to save your reader from boredom, vary your sentences in length and structure. Write *some* long sentences, some medium, but short ones are needed for balance. Good writers maintain this balance though their readers may not be aware of it. Stick to a short sentence on average but vary the pattern as much as possible. Sentence structure is what determines the pace—the rate of movement of all writing. And writing is like a bicycle—it will never fall down unless the pace is too slow. Sentences that 'march' are steady, crisp and move regularly in a predetermined direction. The pace is not hurried. There is a balance without inertia. There is a happy medium between sluggish meanderings of long sentences and irritating rat-a-tat-tat of short telegraphic ones.

Incorrect punctuation can also cause disunity in a sentence. For example, to say 'This is the usual procedure we follow. Although there is no reason why we cannot modify it' is just plain silly. We can say 'This is the usual procedure, although there is no reason why we cannot modify it' or, if we wish to be more emphatic, 'Although this is the usual procedure, there is no reason why we cannot modify it'. A careless string of 'ands' and 'buts' also flattens and weakens writing when they appear between loosely related ideas. Have one clear idea per sentence and make absolutely sure it has a subject and a predicate.

Then make sure all the sentences in each paragraph are closely related to the central topic of that unit in your writing. As a practical point the central idea or topic will often be expressed in a single topic sentence which is the unifying device serving as the key to the whole paragraph. This sentence, by the way, should be constructed so that it says to the recipient *Listen!* It should attract attention and at the same time identify the message. Picture your reader. He is likely to be as busy as you are with a pile of mail in front of him and he will just cast a glance down your piece of paper—'what's this all about'. So to get his attention at once identify the subject, show courtesy, tie down the reference (to his or your previous correspondence, meeting, telephone conversation, etc.) and show action on your part.

With each sentence in each paragraph unified, with each paragraph in your message unified to the central idea of your entire message it will have obvious unity and completeness.

Coherence

We are concerned with the ability to write tersely, to state facts plainly and to convey information intelligibly. To achieve these objects our writing must have, in addition to unity, coherence. The principle of coherence ensures clarity in communication. Coherence is the logical tying together of the several ideas and sub-topics under one main topic in any paragraph. We must set up the logical connection between the several sentences in a paragraph and between the several paragraphs in any written communication. Words, phrases and sentences may be used to provide smooth transitions.

This can be done in several ways. We can repeat key words and phrases. The de luxe 3 litre model is powered by eight cylinders. These cylinders weigh one pound each. We can use pronouns. The de luxe 3 litre model comes in twenty different colours. It is available in every country in the world. Or we can use special linking words and phrases. The new elite 3 litre model has leather seats. Moreover, it also offers you a heated rear window as standard. By way of contrast the previous model in the series offered you neither of these items even as 'extras'.

The clean linkage of ideas prevents double meanings and fogginess. The misreading of messages because of misplaced words, inexact connections and poorly arranged ideas costs huge sums each year. Most of us are careless in the way we express ourselves to one degree or another however professional we may be in other areas.

It has been said 'The man of science makes a fetish of efficiency, yet he shows little regard for the effective use of one of his most important tools—the pen. He believes devoutly in accuracy, yet employs this instrument as carelessly as a small boy employs a gun.'

You must make clear for the reader's benefit precisely what the crux of the situation is. The heart of the problem must be stated and not assumed. You must make clear what observations are pertinent and why.

When writing to anybody on any subject at all you have four things to bear in mind: (1) will your message be received; (2) if it is received will it be read; (3) if it is read can it be easily understood; and (4) if it is understood will your reader take the precise action which you wish taken.

Power

A third basic principle of effective writing is power or emphasis. Emphasis appeals to the ear. It describes to the ear the process of thought. Emphasis should be used in your writing and it can be achieved by position, proportion, repetition, use of figures of speech and by punctuation. To make any noticeable change in the position of a word, phrase, sentence, or paragraph is to make it emphatic if skilfully done. Emphasis by position is one of the chief devices of advertising writers in securing attention. A word will often carry different weight of importance according to its position. The positions of special emphasis are at the beginning and the end of a sentence. By saying more about important items we add to the meaning and emphasize by proportion. Another method by which you can give special emphasis is to repeat an idea—repetition of the word 'honourable' in the speech of Mark Anthony in *Julius Caesar* is a good example.

Emphasis may also be indicated to the eye by punctuation. The most emphatic mark of punctuation is the exclamation point. The full stop is often emphatic too, and so is the question mark. The colon is sometimes emphatic, but the dash is most often used for emphasis in modern writing. Be careful in using punctuation for emphasis. Use it where the emphasis really demands it without trying to make your writing emphatic by its use.

The use of underlining or italics and block letters in words is another method of indicating emphasis to the eye. While this form of emphasis is often necessary remember that the real emphasis should be in the writing itself and not in the manner of its presentation. The use of underlining, italics, etc., should be determined by the writing style, although they will often ensure that there is no misreading. Small words like 'not', 'but', and 'if' are easily passed over and not read at all. These particular words can change the meaning drastically, and it is often necessary to ensure they are not ignored. Remember that when a speaker stresses certain words or ideas you know that he regards these as important. You hear him emphasize. But in your writing the emphasis must be seen.

Precision

The personnel manager of one large corporation says that he sees about two hundred job applications each week. 'The characteristic we look for, and the quality we demand,' he says, 'is clarity.' 'We can get any number of people who can write something that can be understood. But these are not the people we want. The people we want are those who can write something that cannot be misunderstood.'

There are certain things one can say precisely and there are other things one cannot be precise about. For example it would be impossible to describe the difference between the smell of petrol and the smell of oil. But there are items we can be precise about. You often see the % sign misused. This is a precise sign. You cannot mix 65% sand with 35% lime—what is meant is $6\frac{1}{2}$ parts sand and $3\frac{1}{2}$ parts lime. Vague words like 'considerable' and 'large' are of no help to your reader. And neither indeed are 'vogue' words such as 'confrontation', 'pragmatic', 'syndrome', 'dialogue', 'parameters' and the inevitable 'extrapolate'. One of the greatest enemies of precision in technical writing is the continuous use of the abstract instead of the concrete noun. The mark of the virile writer lies in the use of the concrete noun and the active verb. A typical government statement might run like this: 'Her Majesty's Government have been driven to the conclusion, after long and earnest consideration, that this proposition cannot be brought within the realms of practicability in the foreseeable future'. They could say (to quote Groucho Marx) all this in two words—impossible!

Business letters

We all write business letters—managers write them all the time. They may be in reply to enquiries or acknowledging orders. We may be making claims or answering claims. Maybe we are asking for assistance. We may be making a complaint or answering a complaint. Maybe we are asking about someone's creditworthiness. Perhaps we are trying to secure payment of an outstanding account (or even delay the payment of an outstanding account!). A letter may be a reply to a letter received or it may be a letter that calls for a reply. Ask yourself is your letter a specific reply to the questions asked? Will your reader know from your letter precisely what he must reply to?

It is easily forgotten that a letter conveys to the recipient an impression of the writer's personality and of his and his firm's business aptitude. A letter may very well be the first contact a business has with either you or your firm; make it as good an ambassador as you possibly can.

There are five characteristics of a good letter: (1) knowing what to say; (2) clarity and precision; (3) style; (4) courtesy; and (5) appearance.

You quite obviously cannot write a good letter unless you *know exactly what you want to say* to your correspondent. The first essential therefore is to grasp all the necessary facts and arrange them logically and systematically. Writing, as we said earlier, is, like speaking, the expression of your thoughts, and any confusion of ideas leads inevitably to confusion of expression. If necessary, jot down your thoughts on a piece of paper or along the margins of the letter you are answering. Each point in your notes will probably become a paragraph in the letter itself. If you have to answer a number of questions, deal with them one by one, and in the order given. Don't try to answer two questions with one sentence and do not go back to a question once you have answered it. If you yourself are asking questions separate them in the same way. Like any other form of communicating—*Think out what you have to say very carefully.*

Clarity and precision

Having made up your mind about what to say, say it as clearly as possible. Arrange the words and sentences so that they at once convey your exact meaning and nothing else. Choose your words and phrases carefully and use every word in its full and exact sense. This means that you omit any word or phrase that is at all ambiguous. There should be only one possible meaning, and this should be easily understood by the reader. As a rule the first draft of a letter should be longer and more complete than the copy you will eventually send. Better results are usually obtained by condensing a long letter than by expanding a short one. In shortening your letter, condense or eliminate the parts which are least needed for clearness of presentation. Strike out all unnecessary words; replace a phrase with a word where possible and always eliminate the repetition of an idea.

In a very important business letter every word will be analysed and every phrase dissected by the recipient; the more precise the expression therefore, the less likelihood there is of error or misunderstanding.

Style

Letters may be written in (a) the first person singular: 'I thank you for your order for ten suits and am asking that work on these commence immediately'; (b) the first person plural: 'We thank you for your order for ten suits and we are commencing work on these immediately'; or (c) the impersonal passive: 'Your order for ten suits has been received and work is commencing on these immediately.' The first person singular is used by a senior executive of a company where he has authority to bind it and where his opinions obviously matter. A junior member of staff should use the plural whereas the impersonal passive would be appropriate where the subject being written about is very formal.

Mercifully 'business English' has died a natural death in the last ten years but you will occasionally receive a letter saying 'Yours to hand of the 14th inst.' I also get letters which assure me of somebody's best attention at all times and even some from 'Your obedient servant'.

While we have come a long way from these expressions we do still use several that are clumsy.

'We are prepared to offer' for 'We offer'
'Considerable period'—'Long time'
'We are in agreement with'—'We agree'
'Owing to unforeseen circumstances'—'Unexpectedly'
'We have to acknowledge receipt of'—'We have received'
'Furnish all necessary particulars'—'Give details'
'Terminate'—'End'
'Acquaint'—'Tell'

Then we have expressions replete with tautology such as:

'World-wide recognition by all.' World-wide must mean by all.
'Surrounding circumstances.' The word circumstances means things that surround.
'Continue to remain.' Remain means to continue in place.

Avoid all out-moded words such as 'hereat', 'therewith', 'hereto' and thereto'. They are pompous and stilted. You would never use them in ordinary conversation so why use them in letters.

Do not say 'enclosed please find'. 'We enclose' or 'I enclose' is shorter and simpler. Don't say 'enclosed herewith'. If an article is enclosed it must be herewith—and vice versa.

Avoid being flowery. 'The favour of your immediate reply will oblige' is a ridiculous way of saying 'I shall be glad to hear from you by return.'

Be careful about the use of the word 'position'. Often it is used as mere padding. Do not say 'The position regarding the supply of raw materials is deteriorating' when you mean simply 'Raw materials are getting scarcer.' Such phrases as 'in relation to', 'in respect of', with regard to' can nearly always be replaced by the simple words 'about', 'for' or 'of'.

Punctuation is important in letter writing too, as it can completely change the meaning of a phrase or sentence. Punctuation is subject to rules and cannot be done in a haphazard way. If you write short crisp sentences you won't have to worry so much about punctuation anyhow.

Courtesy

As the saying goes, 'politeness costs nothing except in a telegram'. While it is essential to guard against servility in your correspondence a discourteous letter is probably more detrimental than personal discourtesy. The stigma of personal discourtesy attaches to the particular person guilty and may well be forgotten in time. A discourteous letter, however, reflects on the company as a whole, and besides all the immediate damage it might inflict the written word always remains and cannot be denied at a later stage.

Appearance

A good business letter is clearly worth money. The time and trouble spent on writing one are amply repaid by achieving the desired results. Every business letter should be pleasant to read. Stationery for business letters should be of a quality good enough to indicate that the organization does not need to stint money without being extravagant on the other hand. Flashiness should be avoided in headings. For professional firms catering for dignified clients obviously a neat black heading containing only name, address, telephone number and profession being carried on would be appropriate. However, for a firm anxious to establish a reputation for being up to date, in the public relations field for example, it could suggest a lack of imagination and enterprise. Choose a happy medium for your own particular business.

Circulars are so frequently read hurriedly and then thrown away that great care should be taken in their presentation and phrasing so as to draw and hold the attention of the recipient.

An American author once said that a publishing company he knew took so much time and trouble with every aspect of their letters that it was almost more pleasurable to receive a refusal from them than it was to receive an acceptance of a manuscript from any other publisher. Try to frame your letters so that you engender that same feeling.

Memoranda

The memorandum or 'memo' is usually an internal communication. Most companies have a printed form of memo heading and standardized forms. Memos are used to overcome the problem of distance within a company and are used for getting information passed around or up and down within it. They are one way of communicating decisions, instructions and policy and, unlike the telephone, they create a permanent record. Some companies use different coloured paper to denote the origin of a memo.

Memoranda usually lack some of the frills we associate with letters as they are written under more urgent conditions and one is not as conscious of the impression being made. They should nevertheless be written with care and should contain only one basic point. Normally you should begin with a brief background explanation of the problem or situation using just one or two sentences to do so. Then go on to the message itself. Memoranda should always be short and never more than two or three paragraphs. Conciseness is the hallmark of any good memo.

Notices

Notices come in many shapes and sizes and are issued for a wide variety of reasons. They vary from an announcement of the opening of a new branch of a bank, an announcement of an impending bankruptcy hearing to notices of statutory and other meetings. They have certain characteristics that are common to memos in that they are always brief and concern just one central point. You cannot convey a complex message by means of a notice—don't try it. You must be ruthless in discarding all unnecessary wording—only short notices attract attention.

Within organizations they are used by those at the executive level to communicate with those at lower levels. Because of this there is little scope for feedback and care should be taken in the preparation of notices to ensure they do not encourage disruptive or resentful action. Notices are a means of mass communication and their siting is important. Make sure they are situated where everyone who should read them is not just passing by but where they have time to stop and read them. Try to have separate notice boards for different items, e.g., social club, joint council affairs, company affairs, etc. Make your notices as attractive as possible and add some colour if appropriate. Take off the notice board all 'dead' matter at regular intervals.

Dictation

Unless you type all your own letters you will have to dictate to someone! And dictating is an art. Few things ruffle a secretary's feelings more than someone who has no idea what he is going to say and 'er umms' his way through from one turgid sentence to the next.

Remember that short sentences are most desirable. There is a limit to the length of sentence you can hold in your mind at any one time, so you must have the whole sentence ready before you start dictating it. It's no use beginning the sentence with only a vague idea of how it will continue and just hoping it will work out all right in the end. Think of the sentence first; then say it and do not continue dictating until the whole of the next sentence is already in your mind. If you find it difficult to dictate it probably means either you don't prepare properly or your style is bad. There is no doubt though that the fact you are speaking English and not writing it makes you more likely to use 'English as she is spoke'—it will seem strange using words like 'endeavouring', 'envisaging', 'communicate' or 'appreciate' when speaking to your secretary.

Your secretary will appreciate it if you dictate (either in person or on a dictating machine) at normal speed and at an even rate. Don't dictate in spurts. Group your words naturally—don't go on and on. If your secretary is reasonably intelligent she can take care of the punctuation and you can indicate stops merely by pausing. But you must pause in the right places, and it is unreasonable to expect her to transform a badly dictated letter into a piece of perfect prose if you have given her no indication of where you wish quotation marks, capital letters, etc., used.

Enunciate your words correctly—don't mumble. Keep your tone full and sustained to the end of every sentence—don't trail off at the end and don't keep wandering around the room; stay put when you dictate. And as a courtesy to your secretary spell out rare words and be particularly conscious of 'technical' words with which you may well be familiar but your secretary cannot be expected to have them as readily to hand (or mouth) as you. Avoid any facial gestures or expressions that modify meaning in a way that you cannot have conveyed in writing. With every letter you should have a read-back or play-back and always read your letters carefully before signing them. There is a story of a secretary who once typed into a letter the sentence 'I never read letters before I sign them'—and then pointed it out to her boss after he had signed it!

Complete your dictation early in the day to avoid rushed transcription.

Telephones

While not exactly a part of written communication much the same points arise with telephonic communication as arise with dictation. Your gestures and expressions are not seen by the person you are speaking to, certain tones of voice become flattened in transit and misunderstandings very easily arise.

Telephone call structure is theoretically simple. The parties connect, identify themselves to the other together with the subject matter, discuss it, and having made some decision the call is closed.

When you receive a call say who you are or at least who your firm is. Say it clearly—that's the advice of the Post Office. It's also courteous. When you make a call do the same, but if possible point out why you are telephoning—are you returning a call or replying to some correspondence. If your are calling a large organization in regard to a letter do make sure you give the correct reference number; otherwise you may be passed from department to department for what seems like hours.

If you fail to make contact with the person you are calling leave a message and your name and telephone number. It is frustrating to be told six people called but did not leave their name or any indication of what they wanted.

Calls should always be kept as short as possible so that the company's lines are kept clear; besides which STD calls for greater economy in conversations in that calls are charged on a time basis. So once again make sure you have a clear idea of what you are going to say and if you cannot answer a question you are asked don't keep the other person 'hanging on' as we say for ages. Tell him or her you will call back with the information within a few minutes and then do just that.

Reports

Preparing readable reports is an inevitable part of a career in business, industry, education or science. The fundamental purpose of management is decision-making and intelligent decision-making requires sufficient, understandable, useful information. Career advancement often results from adeptness in writing reports lucidly where thoughts are organized logically and presented in an attractive manner. Peter Drucker has said the following in his now famous article entitled *How to be an Employee*: 'As soon as you move one step up from the bottom, your effectiveness depends on your ability to reach others through the written and spoken word. And the further away your job is from manual work, the larger the organization of which you are an employee, the more important it will be that you know how to convey your thoughts in writing and speaking. In the very large organizations, whether it is the government, the large business corporation or the Armed Forces, this ability to express yourself is perhaps the most important of all the skills you possess.'

Authorization

A report is asked for and should not be volunteered. The person asking for it must be definite in his request, and the best way of requesting a report is to ask a question to which the report will be the answer. Knowledge of the source of asking and the reasons therefore will help you keep the work on the report within proper channels of administration and communication and will assist you in writing more pertinently and helpfully. These facts are known as your 'terms of reference'.

Types of report

We should distinguish between four types of report: the routine report; the expository report which is either descriptive or narrative; the interpretative report, which is an interpretation of facts or ideas and the persuasive report which is probably the most difficult of the four to write.

The routine report is one for which there is a precedent; its purpose and format will have been decided when it was first instituted and the preparation and presentation offers little problem. Most routine reports concern financial matters anyway and are usually submitted on predesigned forms which reduce the use of writing and language to a minimum.

The narrative exposition which may be an account of a process of manufacturing or operations is thoroughly concrete and often chronological. It should move, as it is supposed to be a narrative. The reader must know where he is going and why. A narrative exposition should always begin with a summary of what has gone before, as this will help your reader in his effort to grasp further details with more interest and better understanding.

The interpretative report gives meanings to facts, figures and concepts. Do not make the assumption that everyone else will interpret something the way you do. Your reader will be interested not in you but in the information you are passing on. Use discretion therefore in employing the first person.

The persuasive report needs careful stress on fact. Comment on the facts should be subordinate to the facts themselves. Include all the points which you know from your own observation—not assumptions. Be strictly accurate and strictly objective—if you are not, it will easily be seen that your prejudices are liable to lead you to jump to conclusions. It is a well-known legal maxim that 'that which is asserted without proof may also be denied without proof'; it is necessary for you to make quite clear to the reader what assertions you are making. The reader must not have to sort out what is actual assertion and what is an expression of your opinion. It must be quite clear precisely how you are arriving at your main propositions.

Selecting and organizing your material

There are traditional ways of organizing the material that is available to you. You may, for example, choose to organize along lines that are chronological as we have already seen, you may choose a cause-effect organization or perhaps use the problem–solution sequence. Whichever you decide to use, your task of researching, reading, and observing will be greatly simplified if your thoughts are cast into outline form. It will help you tremendously:

    (a)   to make a selective bibliography—one which covers the topics in outline;

    (b)   to read selectively by choosing those parts of articles and books which relate to the specific problem;

    (c)   to observe selectively those matters which are of importance to your report;

    (d)   to look again at your terms of reference; and then

    (e)   to decide on the order of the divisions and sub-divisions.

As your report will always be concerned with facts here is a suggested four-part outline for its preparation:

(1) *Collecting facts*
  (a) reading
  (b) reply from questionnaires
  (c) note taking
  (d) conducting interviews
  (e) observation

(2) *Organizing your facts*
  (a) use a card file
  (b) loose-leaf notebook
  (c) scrap book

(3) *Interpreting the facts*
  (a) definition
  (b) classification
  (c) comparisons
  (d) inferences
  (e) reasoning

(4) Your summary and recommendations.

You have to analyse all your information, and there must be a definite line throughout your material from start to finish. Reject what is irrelevant—reject whatever does not provide basic facts or support them. Make this rejection definite, and return the material to a file where it will not distract you. Then, when this has been completed, carry the stage of sorting further and relegate certain pieces of information to a supporting function to be included in appendices. The basic facts and trends will then remain for the body of the report.

Having followed the two plans of attack outlined already you will be able to produce your report. How are you going to present it?

Form of reports
Title page
Apart from the title this should contain the name of the author, his department, some form of reference letter or number and the date of issue. The title of the report should be short, clear and unambiguous. It should suggest the content of the report and be such that it constitutes the title by which the report will be logically remembered.

Preface

The term preface refers to that which is introductory to the text itself. It is designed to prepare the reader for the treatment of the subject matter. It may draw attention to the particular point or points which you wish to emphasize. Do not confuse it with an introduction which may precede the text at the beginning of the report itself.

Sometimes a preface can be dispensed with and a 'letter of transmittal' is written instead. Since reports are objective and usually fairly formal documents, a letter of transmittal will give you an opportunity to persuade in an informal, personal and direct manner.

Acknowledgements

This is a list of people and organizations to whom you are indebted for help, advice or information. The difficulty with making acknowledgements, though, is that it's hard to know where to start and where to stop without offending somebody. Inside an organization reports will rarely carry acknowledgements, and the reason is that it is considered that all employees of a company have the duty to make their knowledge freely available when requested.

Table of contents

In all but the shortest of reports there should be a table of contents. This will act as a tabular summary. Its purpose is to tell your reader quickly what he can expect from the report. The contents should obviously be listed in the same order in which they appear in the report itself and should have the same wording as the headings in the text. The table should occupy a whole page and represents the chapter or section titles, headings and sub-headings.

Summary

Although the summary should always be written last—when your report is complete—its position in your report is logically immediately following the table of contents. Sometimes a sentence or two will suffice for a summary, but it should never be longer than 300 words. It should indicate the scope of the report and present, with as much precision as possible, the most important results, conclusions and recommendations. The order in which the items are presented in the summary should be the same as that in which they appear in the report itself.

Introduction

From the literary point of view this is probably the most important part of your report. You must get and hold your reader's attention at this point. The first and last sentences will have the greatest impact. Your introduction should provide the reader with the necessary background information including terms of reference etc. It should say why the work has been done, what work was done, what the results were and what they mean, and what your recommendations are.

Method of investigation

This tells the reader how you arrived at the information presented. You may have interviewed people, sent out questionnaires, held meetings, invited written evidence, etc. If you took samples of opinions give an indication of how widely ranged your samples were. Give sufficient information here to enable your reader to have confidence in your methods of investigation and research.

Body

This presents your findings and is the largest part of your report. It is therefore the section that requires the most effort to ensure good readability.

The main divisions of the report or paper may be called chapters, sections, topics or parts. The designation selected should be used consistently whenever reference is made to such a division.

The body will include a discussion, which constitutes the bulk of this section and this states the findings in analysis, synthesis and interpretation. It will provide evidence of the main conclusions, exceptions and opposing theories with adequate explanations of them and perhaps a comparison of your results with the results and interpretations of others. You should emphasize conclusions that modify in a significant way any principle that has secured general acceptance. To prevent misunderstanding it is necessary to define as clearly as possible the conditions to which your conclusions apply. A conclusion should always be stated in such a way as to indicate its range of validity. Very detailed matter should be left for the appendices.

Conclusions and recommendations

The conclusions are not merely endings but are a summing up which state the results of your study. The conclusions are the answers to the questions raised at the beginning of the report. It is always difficult to say what is *the* most important part of any report, but it will usually be the conclusion. (In very long reports conclusions may be presented at the end of each major section within the main body of the report.)

The recommendations, which appear when they have been requested or are otherwise appropriate, state how the conclusions should be used and what other studies should be undertaken or continued. If your report is properly written the reader should be able to anticipate the recommendations from your conclusions. Recommendations should be tactful without being vague, and should always take into account the practical difficulties involved in their implementation together with the financial expenditures needed to effect them.

Appendices

An appendix, while not always essential, is considered to be an integral part of your report. It follows the body of the report and should be treated as the equivalent of a new section. Don't just shovel all the detail and odds and ends into an appendix; appendices should contain only such detailed information of the kind that would interrupt the flow of material in the body of the report and distract your reader's attention. Reference materials of secondary importance may be included in an appendix to avoid making the text of the report unduly bulky. Other items include documents, general reference tables, results of experiments, statistics, forms of questionnaires used, worksheet tabulations, etc.

When the appendix material can be sorted into several distinct topics each topic should be presented as a separate appendix.

Bibliography

Literally, a bibliography is a list of books but this word is used in business reporting to designate all relevant sources, including published and unpublished materials as well as respondents to questionnaires and interview surveys.

Index

In practice an executive report will rarely have an index. Only very long reports should have them or reports which will be used primarily for reference purposes.

Reports in general

There are a few other general points we ought to look at in connection with reports. Obviously, there are short, medium and long reports and a short report can be given in letter form. Again, routine reports would not contain all the above divisions. Use your common sense and take a look at previous reports to assess what form your own report should take.

One item used in most medium/long reports is what we call footnotes. These provide the most versatile method for referring the reader to information outside the text material. They may be used: (a) to acknowledge the source of information; (b) to support arguments; (c) to identify quoted material; (d) to elaborate on the meaning within the text; or (e) refer the reader to other parts of your text. A footnote literally should be placed at the bottom of the page to which it pertains. It should contain all the information needed to indicate clearly the source of the quoted material so that the reader can, if he so wishes, consult it. A footnote should be complete on one page and not carried over to another. Either a symbol or numeral may be used as an index of reference from the text to a footnote, although symbols are usually reserved for indexing footnotes for tabular or algebraic material.

Remember that the primary function of an explanatory footnote is to permit you to insert material which would interrupt the trend of thought in the text, and explanatory footnotes are intended to be helpful and not distracting.

Use of tenses

Any experimental facts should be given in the past tense, e.g., the students *achieved* more in lecture hall A than in lecture hall B. The remarks about the presentation of data should be mainly in the present tense (as should the recommendations) e.g. diagrams showing the percentage yield *are* shown in Figure 3 or the second column of Table 2 *represents* the increase in dividends over the past ten years. Specific conclusions and deductions should be stated in the past tense because this always emphasizes the special conditions of the particular experiments and avoids confusing special conclusions with general ones. For example: wheat *grew* better, under the other conditions of these tests, when ammonium sulphate *was* added to the soil. Don't say; wheat *grows* better when ammonium sulphate *is* added to the soil. When a general truth is expressed it should always be stated in the present tense. Logically general truths are without time distinction. Perfect tense is used when the action or condition is complete either at the time of writing or at the time that is being reported.

When writing your report there are a number of general considerations which you should always bear in mind; e.g. whether or not to include some particular point. Ask yourself is the fact in the report to which attention is drawn reliable? Does it either call for action or demonstrate the effect of action? And, is it big enough to matter? In regard to timeliness ask: How late can the information be and still be of use? What is the earliest moment at which it could be used if it were available? How frequently is it required? Then you need to consider whether or not the recipient is the right person to take action that is needed and which you recommend. Is anyone else jointly interested? What about the presentation. Is the report clear and unbiased? Is the form of it suitable both to the subject and the reader? Perhaps your close interest in the subject has prevented you from allowing for the reader's more limited grasp of the subject. Have you made a good outline plan? Without a proper outline plan no report can succeed. Is your report readable?

Check list on all written communication

In conclusion here is a check list which you would do well to bear in mind when looking at your report in the clear light of day. It also applies to all our writing whether letters, articles, books or reports.

(1) *Inaccuracy*
    (a) Mis-statement or exaggeration of the facts.
    (b) Misrepresentation through omission of fact.
    (c) Errors in data, terms or citations with conclusions based on faulty or insufficient evidence.
    (d) Unreliable mathmatical treatment.
    (e) Failure to distinguish between fact and opinion.

(2) *Inadequate presentation*
    (a) Omission of important topics.
    (b) Faulty order of sections or paragraphs or inclusion of material in wrong section or paragraph.
    (c) Incomplete development of a topic.
    (d) Inclusion of irrelevant or tedious details.
    (e) Passages that are dull, turgid or just plain hard to read.
    (f) Failure to distinguish between what is genuinely new and what is already well-known.

(3) *Style*
    (a) Long sentences (more than two or three typewritten lines) and complicated grammar.
    (b) Incorrect tense or faulty grammar.
    (c) Weak sentence beginnings—a string of weak or meaningless words.

(d) Lack of clarity or long complicated paragraphs.

(e) Wordiness and padding—failure to come directly to the point.

(f) General or abstract words rather than concrete direct words.

(g) Unnecessarily technical language.

(h) Failure to write in the impersonal style which tends to emphasize the subject rather than the report writer and suggests the kind of objectivity appropriate to a reporting situation.

Review

When your report is complete, do one final thing—go over it again at leisure. Get the general flow to see that there is proper transition and proper punctuation. Make sure there are no lapses of grammar. Make sure that it is crystal clear—if it's not, its chances of acceptance will be much slimmer.

The précis

One of the problems of the modern businessman is that he has too much to read and not enough time in which to do so. Mountains of paper cross his desk during the working week including dozens of papers and journals all of which are 'essential' reading! Everybody complains about the problem and the more senior the individual is the more necessary it is to save time and read only what is vitally necessary. Proper information and sufficient of the right information is always needed for correct decisions but few things are more frustrating than to have to wade through reams of unnecessary writing which in itself leads to reduced comprehension.

The task of summarizing is so important these days that there are several companies which actually specialize in publishing abstracts of technical articles in an attempt to keep managers up to date in the business field. It is an important aspect of communication and it is surprising how few people seem to be able to produce a précis of an article under examination conditions. It seems we forget that every time we give someone the gist of a conversation, a film we have seen or newspaper article we've read, we are making a summary. We leave out the inessentials and include what is important, which is exactly what we are supposed to do when making a formal summary in the office or for an examination. (Few people are more boring to listen to than those who go into intricate detail when telling us something quite simple!)

Method of writing a summary

The first thing we have to do is to grasp the theme of the passage we are asked to summarize. You can't possibly make a sensible summary of anything unless you fully comprehend the theme and subject matter of the source material. So you must first read the whole passage and understand it before you attempt to reduce its size. The reduction will be quite considerable—it has to be, if the object of the exercise is to save the reader's time and you will normally be asked to reduce by at least two-thirds of the original and sometimes even to a quarter of the passage or article.

Next you read the passage a second time and underline the pieces which you feel are significant to the theme making sure that all the important points are marked and unnecessary points ignored. From these underlined points you should be able to extract a title for the précis and proceed to make some notes which should cover all the important facts. Normally you will now be able to condense by simplifying the language and using words instead of phrases.

Thirdly we can, from the title, sub-titles and rough notes, prepare a first rough draft of the summary. At this point you must be sure to work from your notes—if you don't you are likely to use the words of the original. Make sure you check the rough draft against the original to find out if you have omitted any essential material. This first draft won't be perfect so it will need editing and you will need to count the words, especially if you have been given a precise number at which to aim. If the examination question has instructions on the precise number of words then don't exceed that number because if you do you will most certainly lose marks. If you are asked to state the number of words used then please do so.

Finally, check your edited draft with the original after you have refined it still further by improving the phraseology, language, etc. Make sure you have retained all the sense and meaning of the original and that your final effort is written in good English. Usually if the tense of the original passage is in the present we use the past tense for the summary and where possible we use reported speech for the précis, e.g. 'The writer said that...' Most business summaries are needed for reports of events in the past and it is just as well to get into the habit of writing in the past tense wherever possible.

The ability to summarize well is one of the most important you can acquire in the area of communication.

Here's a worked example from the examinations of The Association of International Accountants.

Summarize into not more than 100 words the following extract from *The Daily Telegraph*, March, 1979:

Calm Front on Mortgage Rates

Building societies do not panic as easily as they used to, and they approach this week's monthly meeting to review mortgage rates with an air of exaggerated *sang-froid*. Mortgage rates will not go up, and to hear the building society chiefs talk there was never any question of them going up, once the council decided last month not to follow the rise in minimum lending rate which was announced the day the policy group met.

The inflow of funds in February appears to have been just over the £200 million mark, compared with £289 million in January and £254 million in December. This is not as much as the societies need to sustain new mortgage lending at the same level as last year, but when allowance is made for the gradually rising level of repayments and the spare liquidity the societies still have available it is enough to stop any outcry arising from frustrated housebuyers and the building industry between now and the election.

The situation could, however, have become critical if interest rates had not come down again within three weeks. As it is the banks are offering 10½ per cent gross, compared with 10 per cent gross a month ago, and rates for amounts in excess of £10,000 are likely to command a further premium.

National Savings pose a further threat, and it is a fair bet substantial sums were withdrawn to apply for the two new Government stocks last month. All the building societies have been able to offer is a ½ per cent rise in the rate of interest on four-year term shares, which are currently paying 9½ per cent.

Now before you read the précis following, attempt to write one yourself following the advice given already.

Calm Front on Mortgage Rates

Building societies approach this week's review of mortgage rates calmly. Rates won't go up after the council's decision last month not to follow the rise in minimum lending rate.

Inflow for February was just over £200M. January was £289M and December £254M. At this level last year's lending will not be achieved but will be sufficient for buyers and builders until the election.

The fall in interest rates avoided a serious situation as the banks are offering 10½ per cent against the best building society offer of 9½ per cent and there is competition from National Savings too.

Numeric presentation

It would be difficult to imagine any type of management communication totally devoid of numerical content and obviously all businessmen are familiar with numbers. Yet numbers present information of an abstract nature and we should always, if possible, employ some symbolic forms of expression.

There are four generally accepted ways in which we can present numeric information:

(1)   In textual form, which means words plus numbers (Fig. 4);

(2)   Numbers which are set out in logical arrangement called tables (Fig. 5);

(3)   Numbers and/or symbols arranged in their precise logical form, e.g. mathematical equations, chemical formulae;

(4)   Numbers with or without symbols, set against some scale of measurement, i.e. pictorially (Fig. 6).

Textual presentation can be most effective where the message is straightforward; e.g. 50 per cent of the people in this city own two cars. Textual presentation may not be very effective, however, where the entire sentence, or possibly even the entire paragraph, must be read before its meaning is grasped, or where it is difficult to single out individual numbers from the mass, or where it is difficult to make comparisons.

Columnar or tabular presentation has some advantages over purely textual communication in that its logical arrangement makes for clarity. It is more concise in that it concentrates the data by minimizing verbal description because the row and column legends eliminate the necessity for repetition. You must always ensure though that your column headings are as concise as possible consistent with absolute clarity. Quote units always for all tabulated values and align all tabulated figures beneath each other, either by the right-hand number

The Peninsular and Oriental Steam Navigation Company

Statement by the Directors

The half year to 30 June 1979 has been a difficult period with a road transport strike in the United Kingdom, disruptions in Iran and substantial increases in the cost of all types of fuel. The oil trading activities of Energy Division have, however, benefited substantially from the disturbances in the oil industry and Bulk Shipping Division have performed well in improved market conditions. ET&AS have not yet recouped their losses from the road transport strike which had a particularly severe impact on their international operations. Other divisions, taken together, increased their profits. The first benefits of the recent reorganization contributed to the better performance.

The total figure of Group borrowings (£413m at 30 June 1979, compared with £425m at the end of 1978) should continue to fall.

Profit retentions and the crediting to reserves of the balance of ship sale profits referred to in Note 2 have increased Group capital and reserves by £11m to £415m at 30 June 1979.

Since 30 June we have sold our equity interest in the Beatrice Field, subject to Department of Energy approval, for £23.8m and The Bishopsgate Insurance Company Limited for £5.82m. As already foreshadowed, the Board are continuing with the disposal of P&O Oil Corporation and certain other assets which do not give an adequate return or are outside the mainstream of our business.

Some divisions will be adversely affected in the second half of the year by the strength of sterling. Further, increasing competition in the liner trades will have its effect. Nevertheless, the results for 1979, while still inadequate, should show a marked improvement over the 1978 figure.

Interim Dividend

At a meeting of the Board of The Peninsular and Oriental Steam Navigation Company held today, the Directors resolved to pay an interim dividend on deferred stock of 3.0p per £1 of stock for the year ending 31 December 1979 absorbing £4.239m (1978 – 3.0p absorbing £4.239m).

The dividend will be payable to deferred stockholders registered in the books of the Company at the close of business on 30 November 1979. Dividend warrants will be payable on 4 January 1980.

P&O Building, Leadenhall Street, London EC3V 4QL.   5 September 1979

Fig. 4

£ million	1978	1977	1976	1975†	1974	1973	1972	1971	1970	1969
Assets employed										
Bulk carriers and OBOs	27	33	36	37	35	34	22	13	14	15
Cargo ships	131	90	82	81	79	78	71	78	81	81
Chemical and product carriers	29	32	38	38	14	7	1	1	1	—
Container ships	18	22	22	24	26	17	7	8	8	8
Ferries	35	36	37	37	25	17	10	10	3	4
Gas carriers	116	56	31	23	14	14	9	—	—	—
Offshore supply ships and other	7	10	14	10	17	11	5	1	1	—
Passenger ships	41	45	51	49	33	18	10	29	32	32
Tankers	11	11	15	18	20	28	31	32	37	26
	415	333	326	317	263	217	166	172	177	166
Ships under construction	17	60	41	38	36	33	34	38	17	10
Properties (revalued 1973)	155	156	164	167	198	148	28	28	23	22
Plant and equipment	58	51	44	44	37	25	19	24	14	10
Oil and gas interests	14	16	21	16	3	3	—	—	—	—
Interest in leased assets	3	2	—	—	—	—	—	—	—	—
Trade investments	104	113	111	99	97	74	28	23	21	19
	766	731	707	681	634	500	275	285	252	227
Net current assets/(liabilities)	(31)	(16)	3	12	1	42	59	41	31	30
	735	715	710	693	635	542	334	326	283	257
Financed by										
Deferred stock	141	141	141	141	141	61	61	58	52	43
Reserves	260	279	267	249	258	286	150	163	148	155
	401	420	408	390	399	347	211	221	200	198
Preferred stock	3	3	3	3	3	3	3	3	3	3
Outside shareholders	9	10	10	11	9	3	3	11	11	10
Ship sale profits	10	10	12	12	12	3	2	—	—	—
Debentures and loans	299	259	266	268	205	183	114	87	69	46
Insurance funds	13	13	11	9	7	6	4	4	—	—
	735	715	710	693	635	542	334	326	283	257

Fig. 5

Profit

Profit before taxation	18·3	42·5	31·1	22·7	48·5	34·2	12·3	4·9	12·6	12·6
Taxation	9·7	12·8	10·7	9·8	6·4	6·3	0·7	1·3	0·6	0·7
Profit after taxation	8·6	29·7	20·4	12·9	42·1	27·9	11·6	3·6	12·0	11·9
Extraordinary items and exchange differences	(13·7)	(5·0)	4·2	(13·3)	(0·6)	0·7	—	6·0	(0·7)	(2·3)
Profit available for appropriation	(5·1)	24·7	24·6	(0·4)	41·5	28·6	11·6	9·6	11·3	9·6

Appropriation of profit

Dividends – deferred stockholders	9·2	9·2	8·3	9·5	7·1	5·3	7·3	7·0	6·2	5·2
– preferred stockholders and outside shareholders	0·1	0·5	0·1	0·2	0·2	0·2	0·2	0·3	0·3	0·3
Retained (including minority interests)	(14·4)	15·0	16·2	(10·1)	34·2	23·1	4·1	2·3	4·8	4·1
	(5·1)	24·7	24·6	(0·4)	41·5	28·6	11·6	9·6	11·3	9·6
Profit after taxation as % of funds employed excluding debentures and loans and insurance funds	2·0	6·7	4·8	3·2	10·2	7·9	5·4	1·5	5·6	5·6
Earnings in pence per £1 of deferred stock	5·1	20·3	16·1	9·9	32·0	23·1	9·6	2·5	10·8	10·9

†Following the change in accounting date to 31 December, the profit for 1975 covers a period of fifteen months.

The figures for the years up to 1970 do not include undistributed profits of associated companies.

Earnings per £1 of deferred stock have been adjusted for scrip issues.

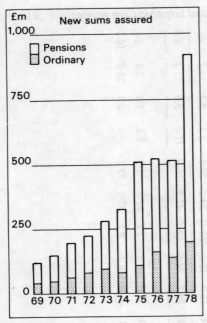

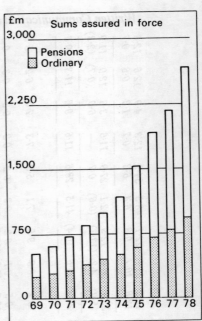

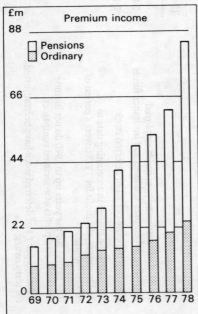

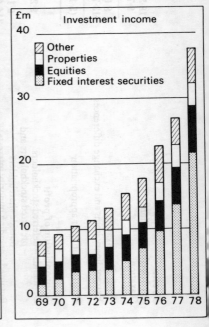

Fig. 6

or by the decimal point. Tables should never be a puzzle, and it is your duty as the communicator to make the interpretation as easy as possible. It is a good rule to bear in mind that if more than three items of information appear together, e.g. three items relative to the same subject of discussion, they should be presented in tabular form. As the eye takes in the columns more easily than rows you should arrange your information vertically whenever possible.

If you can, always avoid large tables. Complex, all-encompassing tables may occasionally be suitable but only for record purposes; in a report avoid them if you can. Be prepared to break up your tables into sets that are easily assimilated. Avoid any appearance of 'clutter' in your tabular presentation and be consistent throughout. Lines should be used sparingly in your tables; it's much better to use extra spacing between columns and between rows unless space really is at a premium.

You also need to consider the attitude to accuracy when preparing tables. Don't quote more than three figures in any column unless you absolutely have to; there's no reason for saying 637.43—just say 637. Ask yourself how small an inaccuracy would be able to alter the significance of the information. Could any small inaccuracy, or several together, make a material difference to the conclusion to be drawn? Remember that the accuracy of any statement cannot be greater than that of the most inaccurate item which goes into it. You judge the degree of accuracy on the basis of three factors:

(1) For what purposes are the figures required? Who is going to use them? What information is he going to look for in them, e.g. just trends, and what action is he likely to take on the basis of the information you are giving him?

(2) What are the magnitudes of the figures? Are they in millions or in tens? Is there a wide range between the largest and smallest magnitudes? Which figures are likely to be related and in what way?

(3) Are the figures going to be subjected to any other mathematical processes? Are they to be added, multiplied, or divided by each other or by any other data and, if so, for what purpose?

Used in conjunction with your text, a tabulation is a valuable means of presenting supporting data in a concise form. Combined with a graph, a table provides the exactitude not normally possible from a mere pictorial presentation.

Graphic presentation

The facts contained in any tabular statement may often be brought out more clearly by using some form of graphic presentation—in the words of Confucius 'One picture is worth ten thousand words'. Graphs, however, should never be regarded as more than a technique for drawing the eye to some particular relationship in order to focus attention upon it more dramatically. It is necessary, for example, for management purposes, for people to grasp the trends or rates of change at the earliest possible moment.

Graphical illustrations are an art form just as much as architecture is, and you would be well advised to call on the services of any art department staff which your particular organization may employ.

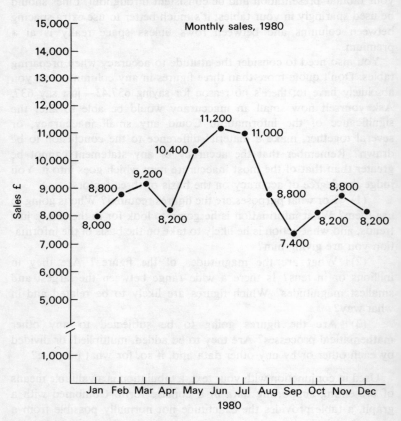

Fig. 7 Simple natural graph

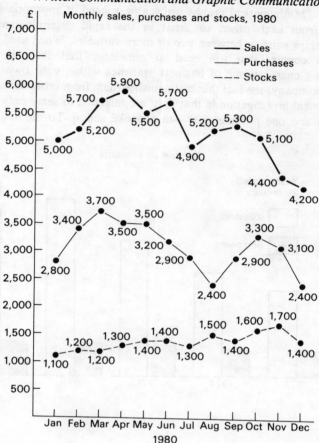

Fig. 8 Multiple natural graph

Graphs save valuable time by disclosing at a glance the trends, results, or seasonal changes as already mentioned but these 'illustrated statistics' should not be used where they add nothing to a tabulation or textual statement.

You have many different forms of graphical statement at your disposal and the most well-known are given below.

(a)   Statistical graphs which depict quantitative relationships in the use of areas, volumes, lengths of bars, heights of columns and slopes of curves.

(b) Mathematical graphs use scales, spaced at appropriate intervals from each other, to assist in the rapid determination of relationships existing between two or more variables. When used in a business context you will need to remember that there is one overriding characteristic of business statistics within your own particular company: the fact that distinguishes them from other branches of statistical investigation is that they are intended to serve only one purpose and one purpose only—to provoke action. To the initiated

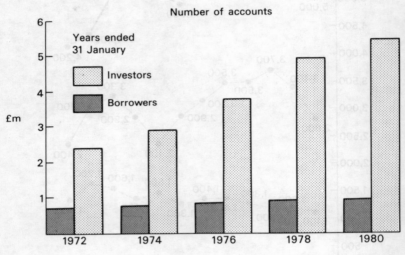

Fig. 9

the graph needs no interpretation at all. (Fig. 7 illustrates a simple natural graph and Fig. 8 a multiple natural graph.)

(c) Bar charts are made up of long rectangles or straight lines drawn to a common scale and of different lengths—they usually depict absolute values or their relative relationships. They are more versatile than area or circle graphs (pie charts), and because of that they have many variants including the sub-divided bar, the paired bar and the grouped bar, which is used to contrast different but related data: income and expenditure, imports and exports, etc. Bar charts present information in a form which enables comparisons to be made very easily (Fig. 9).

Pie charts are widely used to indicate how a particular total is made up and should not normally be used for the purpose of making comparisons (Fig. 10). Occasionally a pie chart is accompanied by a table giving the figures used in the chart itself.

The Gantt chart (Fig. 11) is also a bar chart and was originally used for progressing and production control, but it is valuable wherever it is desired to record achievements against planned objectives and is often

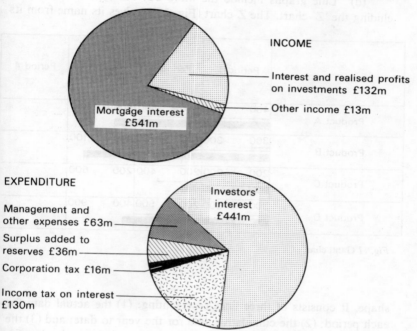

INCOME

Interest and realised profits on investments £132m

Other income £13m

Mortgage interest £541m

EXPENDITURE

Investors' interest £441m

Management and other expenses £63m

Surplus added to reserves £36m

Corporation tax £16m

Income tax on interest £130m

Fig. 10

used appropriately in the field of budgetary control. It consists of two lines, one thick and the other thin, drawn horizontally on a time scale: the figure in the top left-hand corner of each period's division can be the budgeted figure and that in the right the cumulative budget to date. Actual figures are not usually entered, performance being indicated by drawing a thin line across that proportion of the division which represents the proportion of actual to budget—if it falls short the line will obviously fall short; if the target is exceeded a second thin line is recorded above the first until the total length reflects the proportion of budget actually achieved. The cumulative effect is measured by the thick line, which is continuous, the amount of each month's total thin line being added to the existing thick one: this means the position at any point in time can be seen at a glance. The reasons for any interruptions can be noted on the graph by initials or some other code.

(d)   Line graphs include the more obvious type of charts, including the 'Z'-chart. The Z-chart (Fig. 12) derives its name from its

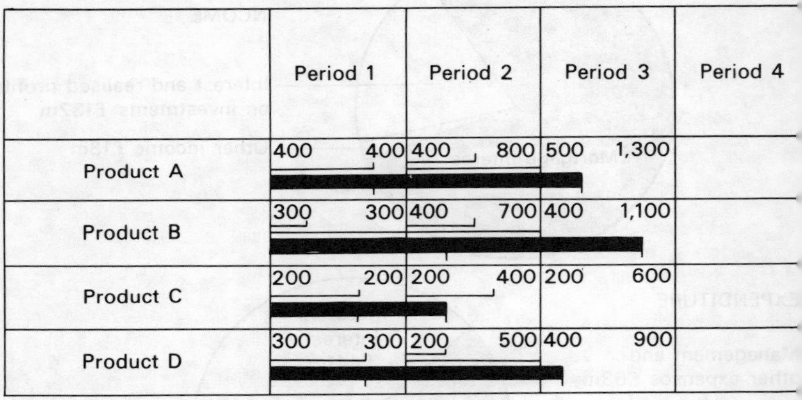

	Period 1		Period 2		Period 3		Period 4
Product A	400	400	400	800	500	1,300	
Product B	300	300	400	700	400	1,100	
Product C	200	200	200	400	200	600	
Product D	300	300	200	500	400	900	

Fig. 11 Gantt chart

shape. It consists of three lines representing: (1) the actual data for each period; (2) the cumulative data for the year to date; and (3) the moving annual total up to and including each period, e.g. the data for the twelve months up to and including the current one each period. From one simple chart it is possible to gain a clear idea of changes from one period to another, the rate of accumulation during the year, and the long-term trend free from short-term fluctuations.

(e)   Pictograms represent facts by symbols and illustrate quantitative relationships. Their utility is restricted to dramatization of simple messages and they are not used much for internal communication with the exception of educational presentations or sales talks. They are, however, as you have doubtless seen many times, used extensively in advertising.

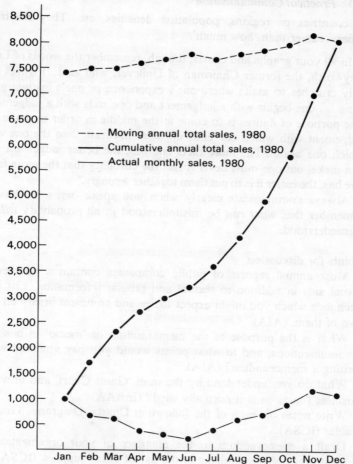

Fig. 12 Z-chart

(f)   Diagrams are visual descriptions that *explain* rather than *represent* and are often used to 'show how some piece of machinery works'. Always keep your diagrams as simple as possible and don't crowd too much information onto any diagram.

(g)   Cartograms are representations and are used largely for simple presentation of geographical data such as the extent of markets in countries or regions, population densities, etc. They illustrate 'where' rather than 'how much'.

In all your graphs and charts, though, remember the words of Lord Heyworth, the former Chairman of Unilever, who said: 'Figures are only crutches to assist where one's experience or one's instinct goes lame . . . one begins with a judgement and one ends with a judgement. The purpose of figures is to come in the middle in order to make the judgement with which one ends up more accurate than the one with which one began. The more facts one has, the better judgement one can make, but one must never forget the corollary that the more facts one has, the easier it is to put them together wrongly.'

Always communicate clearly when you speak, write or draw— remember that what *can* be misunderstood in all probability *will* be misunderstood.

Points for discussion

Most annual reports of public companies contain a number of visual aids in addition to textual and tabular information. List four such aids which you might expect to see and comment briefly on any two of them. (AIA).

What is the purpose of the memorandum or 'memo' in business communications, and to what points would you pay attention when writing a memorandum? (AIA).

What do you understand by the term 'Gantt Chart' and in which business functions is it normally used? (InstAA).

Write notes on each of the following: Charts, Diagrams, Graphs, Tables (ICSA).

Draft a memorandum to the manager of your organization to suggest ways of economizing in the use of office supplies. (ICSA).

13 Meetings and Committees. Discussion Groups and Briefing Sessions

'A camel is a horse designed by a committee'

Anon

Meetings

No business or industrial organization can get along without a large number of meetings (unfortunately!). Meetings, when properly run, are probably the most valuable of a company's means of communication. They are certainly necessary if we are to promote:

(a) Understanding and willing acceptance of the company's policies and procedures;

(b) A correct understanding and tolerance of people's needs and desires; 'two-way' exchange of constructive suggestions and ideas; intelligent co-operation;

(c) Savings of time, of repetition and paperwork.

But meetings cost money. We have to calculate the salaries of those present, the cost of time taken by those who helped prepare for the meeting and produced the necessary documentation and the cost of lighting, heating, ventilating and perhaps even renting the meeting room. It is imperative, therefore, that we use the time spent in meetings profitably, and that the leader and participants achieve the objectives of every meeting arranged.

Meetings vary between these two extremes:

(1) Highly formal, complete with chairman, secretary, agenda, usual minutes and formal rules of procedure;

(2) Very informal—ad hoc meetings about current business often attended by close colleagues on first-name terms.

In the day-to-day working of an organization the first type of meeting is fairly rare. Besides this, there are many good books on formal meetings, whether they be for companies, Local Government or voluntary organizations. And as this book is about communicating anyway, we will content ourselves with looking at the conduct of an informal meeting.

Purposes

I have attended (and conducted on occasion!) meetings that have ended more from sheer exhaustion than for any other reason. I have attended (and still do!) meetings which I regard as a waste of time. The reason often starts with, as indeed in most forms of bad communication, an unclear and inadequate preparation. When you are thinking of calling a meeting the following rules will be helpful:

(1)   Establish a valid purpose for calling the meeting. A meeting may be called: (a) to give information; (b) to get information; (c) to solve a problem; or (d) to secure certain positive attitudes. The leader and participants must know at any point in the conduct of the meeting which of these four objectives is applicable.

(2)   Consider carefully whether the purpose could not better be achieved by some other means, such as a memorandum or a series of telephone calls.

(3)   Consider when the meeting should be held. Make sure all the relevant people are available, the facts or documents are to hand and that the meeting is not being held *after* the decision to be taken thereat should have been taken.

(4)   Establish who should attend. If a decision has to be reached you need people to be present who have the power to make that decision. Sometimes full participation will not be expected, as will be the case when you are calling a meeting to hear a statement of policy, a definition of responsibilities or to receive instructions.

If at all possible you will avoid inviting the 'difficult' member. He is one who talks too much or at length, constantly talks off the subject and is generally quite illogical. He is also impatient and wants a decision without a thorough investigation. He's always unwilling to consider alternatives or compromise, and makes dogmatic unsupported statements; he gives no reasons, and the points he makes always need clarification or illustration. He does not pay attention but always whispers and interrupts. And he always comes to the meeting *you* are conducting! He needs firm leadership, and the use of questions addressed to him will usually go a long way to disciplining him.

Unsuccessful meetings

Before we go on to the conduct of meetings let's look briefly at the problems which occur all too often. First of all, meetings are often held for the wrong reasons, e.g., the organizational structure may not have kept pace with changing needs. *Ad hoc* committees set up to deal with a particular problem sometimes become fixed. Some groups may even be meeting purely out of habit—there may be a regular Thursday morning meeting at 10.00 a.m. with nobody examining whether or not the meeting should still be taking place. There may be inadequate advance information, or faulty composition of the group. The leader may be vague about the subject or purpose. There may be no provisional plan, there may be bad handling of the time factor or physical conditions may be inadequate. Meetings may be held simply because managers feel inadequate. They do not have the courage to make the decisions necessary so they call a meeting; or indeed they may even use the meeting to delay making the required decision.

Meetings may also be unsuccessful because some items had apparently been decided beforehand. Or there may be too much emotion present, while lack of control may allow too many people to talk at the same time. There's always a serious problem if the chairman or leader is biased. Key issues may not be defined nor main issues clarified, so that there will be several red herrings present throughout. Some people may never open their mouths throughout, while others may have no idea at the end of the meeting of what has been decided. Diffident members may even be discouraged or snubbed.

Then at the end the progress may not be summarized, minority views ignored and inaccurate quotation of contributions made. Unsettled points may be left 'in the air', and finally the required action may not be formulated.

Correct approach to running a meeting

First of all see that none of the above problems occurs! Then let's think first about physical conditions. Make sure the temperature of the room is conducive to work—not too cold nor too hot. Ventilation is very important and fresh air keeps participants alert. Noise can be very distracting. There should be a bright atmosphere about the room, with comfortable furnishings—these have a definite psychological effect. Refreshments can revive people, particularly at a long meeting, but do make sure that they are not brought in during a closely-argued discussion. Arrange the seating so that all members can see each other easily—an oval shaped table for larger groups can be suitable and a horseshoe or 'U' table for groups of fourteen or over. If possible, a company should have a few properly equipped conference rooms available on the premises of different sizes and suitably sound-proofed. Of course, meetings do not always have to take place in a room—a few colleagues talking in a corridor may be all that's necessary, and if the right decision is reached in those (or any) circumstances you can be assured the meeting has been successful.

There are really three stages to any meeting—before, during and after.

Before the meeting

You have to decide what you want to achieve through the group of people who will be present. Are you out to sell them some idea, a new company policy, to solve a problem or to secure certain positive attitudes? Do you want them to take a decision that you know they will be committed to without any pressure from you.

Then you have to know the subject being discussed inside out. Do plenty of homework; collect, sort, and arrange all the relevant information. Prepare a workable timetable for your own use, apportioning relative times to major and minor issues. Be well armed in relation to possible questions and/or objections.

Prepare an agenda, which is merely a list of items to be discussed; it covers all relevant points in the right order. The early items should not be controversial and important items should not be left until the very last, at which time some may have had to leave (to attend another meeting possibly!), while those remaining will naturally be tired. It assists pertinent discussion of items on the agenda if they are all divided into sub-sections if appropriate, and all items should be specific and concrete. Often for small meetings held on a regular basis agendas may be dispensed with, but even so, the leader of the meeting should always have one for his own use. Try to have the agenda sent out in good time (obviously statutory meetings have set amounts of notice which must be given), so that all members can themselves be fully informed on the issues to be discussed. If you do send a note with the agenda make sure it tells those attending what the subject is all about and that you are inviting their participation.

Adequate preparation, as in any form of communicating, will greatly help the effectiveness of the meeting, bearing in mind that all of us have opinions, prejudices and attitudes to everything under the sun. And don' forget to have any visual aids or reports ready in plenty of time.

Conducting the meeting

Start on time. Repeat—start on time! Welcome members, especially newcomers. Emphasize the work to be done. State the topic, problem or difficulty with which the meeting is to deal. You may wish to outline the situation giving rise to the topic, and outline what is appropriate for discussion and what it not. Outline the procedure to be followed in the case of groups not meeting on a regular basis.

Define technical terms being used, and remember the subject for discussion must be simply and clearly expressed and all ambiguous words must be clarified. The vague statement of a subject is probably the cause of most futile discussion. It is often a good idea to put the subject before the meeting in the form of an impartial question; one advantage of this is that a question at least provides the framework for the answer.

People called to a meeting tend to bring their immediate problems with them. They may even have decided views on the matters they know are going to be discussed. So you must put them at ease and focus their minds on the purpose of the meeting. An informal call to order is usually all that is necessary to get their attention, and then you begin your brief introduction. After this you may ask a direct question or a question of the group as a whole. The leader must draw out all relevant information, viewpoints and experiences. He or she must make sure that all available information is before the meeting and get further information from members as is necessary. He must stimulate thinking and get the meeting to examine the experience and judgment of all. The member who insists on talking must be interrupted—you can thank him for his seven points and tell him before he continues with the other seven you would like to discuss the ones just made. Everyone—both sides—at a meeting can and should be heard—but not indefinitely. Encourage those who tend to be quiet. Link the speakers together and provide the channel through which they speak. But talk yourself only when you must. Cajole the members into brevity, but try not to choke off discussion until it comes to an end. Wait until you get from the feeling of the meeting that time has come for the particular debate or argument to be wound up. You, as a chairman or leader, are running the meeting, but don't make it too obvious. The top leaders keep the show going and ensure that everyone stays contented and awake, and the finest chairmen are those who use good humour, quiet tact and gentle persuasion.

Summarize the developments of the discussion from time to time and refer to any changes of opinion. State points of agreement and disagreement, state intermediate conclusions as they are reached and make sure

of members' understanding and acceptance of summaries. A particular
ly good time to give a summary is when you notice that uniform
thinking has been reached on one phase of the subject and no really new
contribution is coming forward. There should, of course, be a summary
when each intermediate conclusion is reached. Summaries are also
useful to bring discussion back to the point and purpose of the meeting
when the subject has been extended beyond profitable limits.

Establish the final conclusion reached, state the main points con
tributed at the meeting, mention any minor disagreements, make sure
your summary is fair and that all the members understand it. It should
make clear to people just what they have achieved and what further ac
tion they have committed themselves or the organization to taking.

Try to finish the meeting on time. If this looks like being impossible
then ask the members if they wish to extend the meeting for another
half-hour or so.

At the very end thank the members for their contribution to the group
achievement.

After the meeting

The majority of informal meetings are supposed to lead to changes in
the work situation. You may wish to send a brief summary in writing to
all those present, outlining the decisions reached and the action to be
taken as a result. In any event there should be a permanent record of
what took place. If your summary at the meeting itself has been clear
you won't have people saying 'Oh I didn't think we agreed to that'. Peo
ple do not contest what they have created. Formal minutes and informal
notes also serve as a starting point in any further meetings on similar
subjects.

Committees

A committee is a person or group of persons to whom something is
'committed'. It is therefore possible for one person to form a com
mittee—probably the most effective committee of all! It is usually a small
body of people appointed by a parent body to meet to discuss particular
matters which are defined in its terms of reference. Recommendations
are expected to be made to the parent body, where the committee is an
advisory one. But decisions are expected from a policy committee.
Committees may be homogeneous where all the members are of similar
interests and status, they may be mixed, or joint. Many companies have
joint consultative committees (also called works councils), comprising

representatives of both workers and management and meeting at weekly or monthly intervals. Normally these joint consultative committees do not negotiate conditions of work; they discuss matters of common interest to management and labour such as methods of improving efficiency, safety and welfare. The balance of management and worker participation varies, but it is usual to have equal representation or a slight bias in favour of the workers. These committees are of special value in improving communications within a company.

Most professional institutions, learned societies and voluntary organizations make extensive use of committees. The council would be the main body. There would also be a small executive committee through which most of the business is conducted, and reports thereof would be periodically presented to the council for approval.

There are several advantages of the committee system of management.

(1)   Committee work can be said to be a highly significant feature of modern industrial life and a sign of democratic control in that it is constituted by the free votes of an elected assembly;

(2)   the specialized knowledge of diverse people is pooled for the common good;

(3)   the continuity of the committee is assured regardless of changes in its personnel.

In addition to the joint committee mentioned above there are also standing committees, *ad hoc* or special committees, and the old favourite, sub-committees.

Standing committees are those formed for specified purposes only. These are used mostly by local government and for Parliamentary affairs. County councils, for example, often have a finance committee, a planning committee, a general purposes committee, etc.

Ad hoc or special committees are those formed for special investigations and are usually dissolved when their reports are submitted. The inauguration of a pension scheme or the installation of a computer are items that would be dealt with by an *ad hoc* committee whose members would have special knowledge and experience in these fields. The formation of these committees leaves the parent body free to concern itself with the major business of the institution and with policy.

Sub-committees are occasionally formed to relieve a larger committee of detailed work and their activities are limited to that particular work. Examples are a transfer committee of a board of directors or a finance committee of a governing council.

As well as a good means of communication there are intricate psychological and social motives underlying committee work. Executive control by individual to individual is sometimes fraught with complicated emotions and some inhibitions. But sitting down with others round a table in committee provides an opportunity to shed those inhibitions. People are there to voice opinions, exchange ideas and contribute to the decision and there is therefore a kind of anonymity which pervades committee work.

Committees generally tend to be reasonably formal, with their own rules as to quorums, proposals, resolutions, minutes and all matters of election and procedures. They make a very large and valuable contribution to industrial, local governmental and professional life of the United Kingdom and embody a proud tradition of service.

Discussion groups

In our society more and more of the daily operations of business, education and government are being directed by groups of people—committees, boards, councils, and conferences. Certainly any business or professional man spends much of his time participating in discussions; in fact, his effectiveness in his job may be very largely determined by his skill in discussion. Although discussion varies in method from group to group, the following should serve as a good working definition: discussion is a co-operative process by which a group of persons exchange and evaluate ideas and information about a mutual problem in order to understand or solve that problem.

There are generally two purposes of a discussion group which may be independent or inter-related: (a) to exchange ideas or opinions; and (b) to reach an agreement or make a decision. The least any discussion can do is to inform each participant of the other members' knowledge and opinions about the subject under consideration. Sometimes this is the only purpose of the discussion but often the exchange of ideas is merely a preliminary to making a decision. In either case the pooling of information and the expression of the divergent opinion are very valuable methods of getting a broad understanding of the problem and of providing a sound basis for making a decision. If it is desired to reach an agreement there is no doubt that through the give-and-take of discussion individual beliefs are often modified and a consensus reached. If a consensus should prove impossible at least the range of disagreement may be sufficiently narrowed so that a clear understanding of the remaining basic differences are arrived at.

The various types of discussion group with which you and I may be expected to be involved are: Study groups, Committee Meetings, Panel discussions, or Symposium discussions.

A study group is normally quite an informal affair. A speech or lecture is given, after which there is a mutual exchange of information. The ideas and information exchanged means that those present learn something from each other as in the case of conventions or seminars where men and women in the same business profession tell each other of experiences they have had or detail the results of their research or methods of dealing with common problems.

We have already dealt with Committee Meetings.

Panel discussions

Where a group is too large to engage in effective discussion or many of its members are too uninformed for such a discussion to be mutually profitable, a small group—usually about three to six individuals—often discusses the problem on a platform before a larger group. The individuals in the panel are chosen because they are well informed on the particular topic and can supply the facts needed for intelligent discussion or because all of them are known to represent points of view held by a considerable part of the audience and can act as spokesmen to express these viewpoints.

The symposium discussion

Very common in America. They arise where a small group of people usually four or five give a series of short six or seven minute speeches each presenting a different viewpoint or aspect of the particular subject being discussed. They are common at large conventions where experts are asked to talk on varying subjects or several aspects of the same topic and they are also used to report the findings of various groups attending a conference.

Both the symposium and panel discussion are often followed by an open forum, where the participants answer questions put by those in the audience. The general principle of the symposium and panel discussion is that one small group do most of the talking while the larger group listens and asks questions.

When leading a discussion, state the topic, problem or difficulty with which the meeting is to deal, and outline the situation giving rise to the topic problem or difficulty. State the purpose of the meeting so that everyone present knows what is appropriate for discussion and what is inappropriate. The vague statement of the subject is probably the cause of most futile discussions. The subject must be simply and clearly expressed and all ambiguous words must be defined. Some subjects at meetings are put so broadly that it is extremely difficult to know just what the field of enquiry is.

Then throughout the discussion there must be order. This does not necessarily imply great formality; in fact in small discussion groups formality would be entirely out of place. Order does require, though, that only one person talks at a time and that each member be consistently courteous. Some definite procedure must be followed as I have already indicated, otherwise the discussion wanders too far afield. Every member must co-operate. If each person insists on having his or her own way the discussion will get nowhere. Members of the group must have a willingness to discuss points of view other than their own and there must be some agreement to compromise. There are no doubt occasions when compromise is neither desirable nor possible but reasonable compromise should always be the objective. The more each member knows about the other members the more they will be able to judge the value of their remarks and the better they will be able to secure the approval of their own.

As a leader of any discussion you should always: (a) prepare a timetable; (b) outline a clear introduction; (c) know the final objective; (d) know the intermediate objectives; (e) frame appropriate questions; and (f) quote any relevant case examples.

For the ordinary member of a discussion group you must learn that, while if you keep quiet, you will learn a good deal, you will not thereby help solve the problem. Develop, therefore, the ability to present your ideas clearly and tactfully and learn to bring them in at the most strategic time. Don't delight in scoring points off your colleagues—a committee meeting or discussion group is not a game. And always do your homework first.

Briefing sessions
Briefing sessions are a systematic and checkable method of downward communication involving managers and supervisors at all levels. All of those who are intimately concerned with time spent in the Services know what 'de-briefing' groups are and the principle holds good in an industrial situation. They bring people together in small groups under their immediate boss in order that any situation can be explained to

them face to face. Consequently they, in their turn, are able to ask questions and so understand not only what is happening but why. They help keep everyone in the picture and are ideal in a scattered organization.

The key person in explaining management's point of view is the immediate supervisor, and while it takes supervisors' time, it is necessary for it to pay dividends. By using supervisors to explain management policies the supervisor is made a more effective boss, because he who communicates is he who leads. At a time when more and more supervisors are joining trade unions it is essential to bring home to them, whether or not a union represents them to negotiate conditions of employment, that this in no way affects their vital role as the first line of management.

The items for briefing are those which affect a man's will to work effectively. They will therefore be items about the job-quality, safety, changes, progress, performance of the group; and those things which affect all workers personally—promotion, employment policies, security, and so on.

Normally a form is given to each supervisor with the items to be briefed printed clearly thereon with a space left after each item for a note of any points which the briefer must especially emphasize. Briefing should not only be checkable but be checked which is best done by managers sitting in now and then on a briefing session. Briefing sessions should take place with no fewer than six nor more than twenty persons present. This greatly facilitates the number of questions and answers which can be handled during the session.

More and more large companies are using briefing sessions to inform their workers of matters affecting their work and are very complimentary of the results being obtained.

Points for discussion

What is the value of sub-committees?

'A committee is a body of people who individually do nothing and collectively decide that nothing can be done'. How far do you agree? What guidelines would you observe in order to make the best use of a committee meeting? (ICSA)

Much, though not all, of the responsibility for the effectiveness of a board or committee meeting can depend on the chairman.

What can an individual member do to help make a meeting as effective as possible? (InstAA)

As committee secretary, what steps would you feel you should take in preparation for a normal monthly committee meeting? (AIA)

Having accepted the Chairmanship of either a professional, trade or social organization, what preparations should you undertake in order to carry out your duties satisfactorily? (AIA)

14 Public Relations and the Social Aspects of Communications

'If everybody minded their own business' the Duchess said in a hoarse growl, 'the world would go round a deal faster than it does'

Alice in Wonderland

Like inflation accounting, public relations is easier to define by saying what it isn't rather than what it is.

Public relations, therefore, is not:

A letter from a finance company saying, 'I'm a computer and I'd like to say hello';

A press release 'Plans are in hand for the replacement of the Stock Exchange film, My Word is My Bond, which is now out of date';

A statement by the chairman of a public company at their annual meeting revealing, 'The major event of the year was the appointment of a new managing director. As a substantial shareholder, I would say the company is to be congratulated on its good fortune. As his father I commend him to your indulgence.'

Public relations *pace* the Duchess, is helping everybody to mind everybody else's business in order to make the world go round a deal faster than it does at the moment. In other words, PR is communications; communications is participation; and participation means progress.

There are, of course, plenty of other definitions.

The Institute of Public Relations maintains that PR is 'the deliberate, planned and sustained effort to establish and maintain mutual understanding between an organization and its publics'. Herbert M. Baus claims it is a 'combination of philosophy, sociology, economics, language, psychology, journalism, communication and other knowledges into a system of human understanding'. For my money, in spite of so much evidence suggesting it is merely Dale Carnegie writ

133

large, I believe public relations means goodwill. And goodwill is an asset to be maintained and developed just the same as any other major asset of a business.

As such, therefore, public relations can profit every single division—or activity—of a company. It is not exclusively the preserve of the sales division. Nor is it simply aimed at the mass media. Public relations is a total company service, capable of using every communications means at its disposal, to maximize that most intangible of all assets: goodwill. For, like it or not, it is now an irrevocable fact of commercial life that no person, let alone a public company, is an island. Every individual and every corporate body has its relationships and responsibilities. And the power of public opinion exists to hammer them into submission. In other words a company should behave like a good citizen in business.

Public relations, therefore, is the corporate discipline which ensures not only that a company behaves like a good citizen but—and this is natural for a commercial organization—the company is seen to be acting like a good citizen and obtains the necessary recognition for it. After all, when John D. Rockefeller started handing out pennies to the kids in Central Park he took a photographer with him!

The public relations practitioner, therefore, treads a dangerous yet vitally important path in commercial life to-day. For while he must be a good and happy member of the corporate team, he must continually remind his colleagues of their relationship with the outside world. In other words, he is a cross between a consumer's advocate and a devil's advocate.

Public relations and general management

Don't let us beat about the bush. The public limited company is in business to make a profit. There is nothing wrong about that. A profitable company is an asset to everybody involved. What counts, however, is the way in which it makes its money. The profit from slave-trading might have been substantial, but it was still wrong.

The public relations orientated company will aim to strike the right balance between its shareholders, its employees, its customers and the public at large for two reasons. First, because it is so obviously the right thing to do, and the second, because the public generally will no longer tolerate any activities to the contrary—and it is dangerous for any commercial organization to go against the public will.

Public relations and a company's financial relations

The Stock Exchange, The Takeover Panel, this and that Company Law; every day there are more and more regulations governing the financial relations of a company. Just as companies have a duty to the general public, they also have a duty to their own shareholders and the investing public generally. Sir Martin Wilkinson, former chairman of the Stock Exchange, London says, 'Communications with the shareholder and the investing public generally must be a continuous and continuing process designed with a clear understanding of the needs of those for whom it is designed and supported by the company making the communication.' In other words, keep the market informed about what's going on.

The company won't suffer either. Such a policy will ensure the shares reflect the financial and trading position as well as the future prospects of the company. It helps the company's reputation. And, of course, it helps money-raising activities.

Public relations and a company's internal relations

Gone are the days of Henry Ford when it comes to internal relations. For Henry Ford used to lay the law down on employee communications. 'It's not necessary for any one department to know what any other department is doing', he used to say. Today it's different. Participation is writ large. Professor Scot Meyers, a psychologist with Texas Instruments, claims it is in every company's interests to develop that vital sense of commitment among their workforce. Employees want more from their work than just a fat pay packet. Hence the flood of house journals and internal bulletins, which ensure better means of communication. Gradually, the first painful steps towards some form of genuine participation are also being taken. Quarterly report-back meetings are beginning to appear in some companies. The wraps are being taken off some of the less important financial details. Joint decisions between management and labour are being taken.

Public relations and a company's position in the community

At the lowest level, this is the world of the parish pump. At the highest, it can cover a company's relationships with the government machine and the legislators themselves.

A company's responsibilities should start with the local communities in which it operates and range to the whole of society itself. Employees should be encouraged to take part in local affairs, sit on local committees and assist local charities. On the wider stage, the company itself must be responsible completely for the social consequences of its actions and activities towards society and the environment as a whole.

At the same time it must ensure its contacts with government for two reasons. First, to educate the government to the realities of any situation. The government machine is arguably the largest single and most powerful machine in the country. Everything it does affects somebody. To let it run riot without the benefit of front-line experience is to invite disaster. Second, to ensure the company is not adversely affected by any government decision taken in a vacuum.

Public relations and lobbying

This is a delicate area. In the demoniac world of PR mythology, this is the nether region of coffee tables and smoke-filled rooms. In the real world, it is simply the age-old custom of hiring an outside expert to carry out an assignment that cannot be handled by a company man.

The crunch, of course, hinges on whether the lobbyist reveals his function or not. The nearest description one can get to formal lobbying, it seems to me, is to misquote Burke's famous definition of a Party: '. . . a body of men united to promote by their joint endeavours a sectional interest upon some particular principle in which they are all agreed'. The definition offered by the United States Federal Regulations of Lobbying Act, Section 307, is no better.

'The provisions of this title', it states, 'shall apply to any person (except a political committee as defined in the Federal Corrupt Practices Act, and duly organised State or local committee of a political party), who by himself, or through any agent or employee or other persons in any manner whatsoever, directly or indirectly, solicits, collects, or receives money or any other thing of value to be used principally to aid, or the principal purpose of which person is to aid, in the accomplishment of any of the following purposes: (a) The passage or defeat of any legislation by the Congress of the United States, (b) To influence, directly or indirectly, the passage or defeat of any legislation by the Congress of the United States.'

And, of course, it has been riddled with loopholes.

Supreme Court decisions have virtually deleted 'indirectly'. 'Solicits, collects or receives' was held to mean what it said—which was surprising. Spend your own money and you're safe. Spend somebody else's and you're in trouble.

Pressure groups and lobbies, I believe, are essential to our form of government. Not only do they provide a constant monitor on the activities of the executive, they also allow different people to contribute to the particular issue under debate. But I strongly believe we have the right to know who is behind any pressure group. Formal lobbyists should come clean and tell us who they are; what they are fighting for; and how they are supported. Members of Parliament, especially, should let us know when they are lobbying for a particular cause; who engaged them; and the nature of remuneration, if any. When we know the facts we have nothing to be afraid of.

This is a broad programme. To implement such a programme for a single company is a major undertaking. It is also a major responsibility. Inevitably that means society as a whole has a duty to ensure such a programme is carried out in a fair and open manner by responsible, trained and informed individuals.

Until the day the police form a special PR Squad to stand alongside the Fraud Squad, I will be accused of jumping the gun or whatever the equivalent is of seeing Reds under the beds. But I firmly believe society has a right to know the length and breadth of any PR guidelines.

Points for discussion

Give a definition of Public Relations in its simplest form.

How does a company's public relations policy interact with its financial relations?

Why should public relations ensure a business has contacts with government?

What is meant by lobbying?

Do you think that lobbying is advantageous in a democratic society?

Describe the ways in which the Press can be of help to a business or industrial organization. (ICSA).

15 The Background to the Mass Media

'Now for the evidence' said the King, 'and then the sentence.'
'No!' said the Queen, 'first the sentence, and then the evidence.'
'Nonsense!' cried Alice, so loudly that everybody jumped, 'the idea of having the sentence first!'

Alice in Wonderland

You pays your money. And you takes your pick.

The mass media is either the most successful business in the world for in straightforward marketing terms it has achieved not only mass saturation of its potential market but a life-long hold on its customers as well. Or it is quite simply, as author Malcolm Lowry wrote, intellectual male prostitution of speech and language.

Similarly, the concept of the freedom of the press. Either your heroes are Milton, Locke and John Stuart Mill. Or you're a disciple of George Orwell's nightmare world of Newspeak, Thought Police and Doublethink.

The mass media is like one giant balance sheet. It is either an asset or a liability. It cannot be both.

A brief history

The mass media was born on March 11th 1702. The *Daily Courant*, printed in an office just off Fleet Street, was the first daily newspaper to be published in the world. Before then breakfast tables were littered with leaflets and newsletters. Papers and journals were being published on an occasional basis: once a week; once a month or whenever there was anything to complain about. The Daily Courant turned a hobby into an industry that is even now still trying to cope with our insatiable demand for news, news and still more news.

But the Daily Courant was a far cry from newspapers of today. There was little news; no features and a complete absence of facts! The Act of Union between England and Scotland which put a halt to the demarcation dispute started by Edward I came and went without a murmur. The political downfall of Marlborough, still glowing with the success of his military victories, failed to warrant a single paragraph. And the decisive victory of the House of Commons over the House of Lords, which set the seal on the constitutional struggle that had blazed fearlessly since the Restoration didn't even creep into the Stop Press. The Daily Courant had forged the ultimate deterrent of the freedom of the press. But it was frightened to use it. Instead it stuck to secondhand news and avoided opinion at all costs.

The weekly press, however, stepped into the gap. Swift, Addison, Steele and, of course, Defoe took the great political issues of the day to the country and rocked public opinion far more than a thousand investigations by the Sunday Times Insight team. If Swift, Addison and Steele were the first political corespondents, Defoe was the first all round news reporter. He introduced on-the-spot reporting. He described all scenes and all men. And he was, by comparison, a moderate. He was the Alan Whicker of the 18th century news media.

The floodgates were now open. Political journals, social journals and literary journals were being launched by the week. Perhaps the greatest of them all was Addison's *Spectator*, that unique combination of literary journal and daily newspaper combined.

Within two weeks circulation hit 3000 copies a day. For special issues it jumped often as much as 20,000. The *Spectator* was the first to master the basic tenet of all journalism: Information + Entertainment = Influence + Commercial success.

The financiers, however, were slow. It took nearly another two hundred odd years before the appearance of a daily financial newspaper. The *Financial News* was launched on January 13th 1884. The *Financial Times* came on February 13th 1888. Both editors, Harry Hanan Marks and Douglas Gordon MacRae, were convinced of the need for a comprehensive daily service of financial and industrial news and comment. They were on target. But they had difficulty proving their case—until the great Kaffir boom burst in 1895. Immediately everybody wanted information. And they wanted it fast. A flood of new flotations and prospectuses boosted their circulations enormously. At the same time, more and more people were becoming interested in financial matters.

Financial journalism had arrived. But we still had a long way to go before the newspaper industry became the mass media as we know it today. Although there were nearly thirty daily newspapers being published in London and hundreds more up and down the country when Alfred Harmsworth founded the *Daily Mail* in 1896, there was not one newspaper large enough to be quoted on the London Stock Exchange.

The newspaper industry was being engulfed by the sweeping political, social and techological changes of the time. Instead of seeking the role of the mass media, the press found it was being thrust upon it. The second Reform Act had started the trend when it broke, once and for all, the upper classes hold on the levers of power and enfranchised one million town labourers in 1870. The Third Reform Act in 1884 added another two million agricultural labourers to the voters rolls. The trend could no longer be reversed. Politics had become the staple diet of the country. If you couldn't actually take part, you could at least shout at the players or change your team at election time.

And as the effects of the Education Act of 1870 began to be felt, the number of spectators began to grow. Politics was no longer a club affair. It had become national league. It was open to all comers.

Technology was also making its mark. The new telegraph system meant instant news. Instead of waiting weeks for the latest engravings to arrive by ship from gentlemen correspondents scattered across the far corners of the world, the news was now pouring into Fleet Street as it happened. And the development of the railways meant Fleet Street could also despatch its newspapers all over the country faster than ever before. The newspaper industry was becoming a mass media and London was becoming the centre of the newspaper industry.

But the breakthrough was sealed with the development of the rotary press. Only a few years earlier in 1896 the linotype machine had increased the rate of typesetting no less than six times. Now the rotary press meant newspapers could print thousands of copies an hour.

News from all over the world could pour into Fleet Street; be printed overnight and despatched throughout the country to an increasingly literate and politically conscious readership by early morning.

But there is more in life than politics. And the man who realized that people also wanted to be entertained at their breakfast table was the fabulous Alfred Charles William Harmsworth, later Lord Northcliffe.

His genius was to take the staid, old, stuffy newspapers and make them fun. Not for him the ponderous prose of Whitehall or the clichés of one official spokesman after another. He believed in life and laughter and all the razzamatazz he could drum up. His newspapers were for the man in the street, not for the civil servants in their wing collars. And the circulations of his newspapers proved it day after day. Within just three years of launching the *Daily Mail* he had to open additional printing facilities in Manchester. Sales soared past the million mark. The *Daily Mail*, launched on only £15,000 was one of the wonders of the world.

Newspapers would never be the same again. And Lord Northcliffe, the master of the sensational story and even more sensational headlines, had turned them into the mass media.

The mass media to-day

Let us start with the figures. Overall there are more than 6500 newspapers and periodicals currently being published in this country. They range from the august *Financial Times*, through the *Beano*, to the typical company house magazine.

There are 142 daily and Sunday newspapers, the number having remained constant for two years, although it is still a dangerous low from the 147 total achieved in 1963. But it is by no means guaranteed. Most national newspapers have a question mark hanging over their heads. The *Sun* is credited with the fastest growing circulation. The *Financial Times*, part of Lord Cowdray's Pearson Longman press empire, is said to be the only national paper making anywhere near the financial return expected from industry generally. The other trend affecting the national press is the inevitable swing towards London. Gone are the days when the individual regions could support two, if not three, daily papers. Today only London can support two evening newspapers.

The morning newspaper roll-call, therefore, would be as follows: London, 14; the rest of England and Wales, 15; Scotland, 5; Northern Ireland, 2; and the Republic of Ireland, 4. Neither the Isle of Man nor the Channel Isles boast their own daily, which says something about the economics behind today's newspaper industry. The evenings seem more healthy with no less than 22 per cent hitting record sales figures in recent months.

The big London-based newspaper groups decided a while back that the future—and the profit—was in the provinces. Each, in turn, has built up their own regional empire led by the one-time buccaneering Lord Thomson. Thomson Regional Newspapers have identified the major regional growth centres and jumped in with their own regional newspapers. In some cases they have acquired a regional base. In others, they simply started from scratch.

Overall, therefore, there are more than 80 evening papers in the country. London has 2; England and Wales, 72; Scotland, 7; Northern

Ireland, 1; the Isle of Man and the Channel Isles, 2; and the Republic of Ireland, 3.

With the gradual decline of the *News of the World* from its one-time pinnacle of over 8 million circulation, the Sunday press has not been at its peak for years. The qualities are holding their grip, although in money terms a number are in trouble. London has maintained its compliment of 7; England and Wales have 3; Scotland, 7; Northern Ireland, 1; and the remainder, 5.

On the weekly scene, the figures are bleak. The total has come down from 1290 papers to 1186 in ten years. What good news there is, is difficult to find. But it's there all the same.

The *West Highland Free Press* was launched in the Isle of Skye in May, 1972. As befits Scottish Nationalists it runs some articles and features in Gaelic.

Periodicals are the big league. There are more than 4400 published weekly, fortnightly, monthly or even quarterly. They range from the *AAFAQ*, published monthly at 15p, to the *Zoological Journal of the Linnean Society*, quarterly at £10 per annum. And they increase and multiply at an alarming rate. Ten years ago, for example, there were only 3994. But, of course, they have their failures.

Candida, a bright, glossy woman's magazine closed after seven issues. Another magazine, *Club*, which tried to be a teenage *Playboy* crashed after 18 months when it finally discovered teenage tastes were much the same as the rest of the population when it comes to some subjects rather than others.

The big, recent success, of course, is *Cosmopolitan*, the liberated magazine for the liberated woman. Launched with an initial circulation of no less than 300,000, it soared to over 400,000 within a single month.

Not far behind—in circulation figures if not in content—come the comics or juvenile weeklies, depending on your prejudices. Sales soared to a combined total of more than 5 million copies a week in recent months.

A word about house journals, another growth centre. Up from 666 ten years ago to more than 798 to-day, they range from *BOAC News*, which is published free every week to the staff, to the *Ystra Rally*, the newsletter of the Dukeries Motor Club.

In some quarters, they are seen as an invaluable aid to industrial relations. Lord Robens has gone as far as saying that while he was chairman of the National Coal Board, their 215,000 circulation *Coal News* had been 'the biggest single factor in our success in industrial relations . . . If industry in this country realized how cheap it is in terms of industrial relations, they would have done a lot more about it.'

The majority of house journals are circulated free to staff, if not at a nominal charge. Few companies expect to make a profit out of them.

Similarly, they are wary of the degree of influence they have in presenting company information. As a result, most house journals are controlled by a management committee, composed equally of management and trade unions, which in turn guarantees the complete editorial freedom of the publication. In fact, in editorial terms most of the house journals have more freedom than the greatest newspapers in the country.

Nowhere in the world, therefore, is there a greater range of mass media and diversity of interests than in this country. Few countries have national newspapers let alone a choice of national newspapers covering the social and economic spectrum as we do.

The question facing the industry to-day, however, is how long can it survive?

Already we have seen one spectacular failure after another. The *News Chronicle* crashed with well over one million circulation. The *Daily Sketch* disappeared into its stable-mate, the once glorious *Daily Mail*. And to-day, it is claimed, there is not one single national newspaper making money. Even the *Financial Times*, for so long the only newspaper to make a profit, has succumbed.

The reason, of course, is costs. And central to any discussion of costs in the newspaper industry is the question of advertising. For under the present system publishers rely on the revenue from advertising to cover their costs. For a popular newspaper with a large circulation, this can be as little as 40–50 per cent. For a quality Sunday, it can be as high as 80 per cent. But it is still not enough. While advertising can be affected so easily by the economic situation, it is no wonder newspaper finances are in such a state.

Yet the amazing thing is that few journalists ever consider the role of advertising in newspaper production. Like Northcliffe, they tend to think of it as encroaching on their news space instead of being the paymaster it really is. Lord Thomson, however, has begun to change this with this emphasis on the need for advertising around which, he has said, the news can be printed.

But there are more insidious threats to the press—from the inside.

The editor of the *Evening Standard*, Charles Wintour, claims in his book, *Pressures on the Press: an editor looks at Fleet Street*, that the latest threat was coming from trade unions trying to prevent the publication of news and views they resented.

The Editor of the *Sunday Telegraph*, Brian Roberts, has pointed to a 'two-fold threat to the editorial prerogative' first, from employees, believing they could edit a newspaper better than any single editor, and second, from the suggestion of Mr Anthony Wedgwood Benn, MP, that newspaper workers should use the threat of industrial action to censor the contents of the publication which employed them. For Mr Benn had told the Labour Party conference on October 6th, 1972, that 'trade unionists who work in the mass media would remember that they too are members of our working-class movement and have a responsibility to see that what is said about us is true'.

The challenge is on the table. There is no shortage of people ready to take it up.

Yet while the debate about the freedom of the press continues, the fact remains that only four out of our eight national newspapers could survive in their own right without support from other newspapers or companies within their groups.

The *Sunday Telegraph* does not make a profit. It is subsidised by the *Daily Telegraph*. Similarly *The Times*, which is subsidised by Lord Thomson's other interests. The *Daily Mail* is subsidised by Associated Newspapers' other activities which include everything from taxi cabs to North Sea oil. *The Guardian* is carried by the prosperous *Manchester Evening News* while the *Daily Express* only manages to survive with the help of Beaverbrook's regional newspapers.

The dilemma, therefore, is obvious. The constitutional role of the press can only be upheld thanks to the generous aid given by one or two selected and totally unrepresentative individuals. Few people would agree that this is the ideal solution. So far, however, nobody has come up with the perfect solution. And it's not for want of trying.

One of the earliest proposals was for an advertising levy which would be set against the most successful newspapers in terms of advertising revenue and force them to re-distribute some of their gains to the less well-off newspapers.

Another idea was simply to limit the amount of advertising space in each newspaper. Further variations include waiving all VAT as far as newspapers were concerned; setting up a newspaper redundancy fund, along the lines of the docks board, which would provide Government money to re-train newspaper workers surplus to requirements. Others have suggested newsprint subsidies while there is a vogue at the moment for the Government to provide the basic machinery while the management of the different newspapers was virtually up for auction once every two to three years.

The problem with all these proposals, and variations on them, is that they tend to shield the less successful without in any way at all actively helping the needy newspapers. But at the end of the day, therefore, they are likely to remain where they are: proposals. For the harsh reality is that while the present plight of the press is a problem, it will be even more of a problem to put it right.

In any case, newspapers might not remain in their present format for many years to come.

The Times is read by the people who run the country.
The Guardian is read by the people who would like to run the country.
The *Financial Times* is read by the people who own the country.
The *Daily Telegraph* is read by the people who remember the country as it used to be.
The *Daily Express* is read by the people who think the country is still like that.
The *Daily Mail* is read by the wives of the men who run the country.
The *Morning Star* is read by the people who would like another country to run the country.
The Sun—well, they found a gap in the market!

The future

Any time over the past 500 years William Caxton or Johann Gutenberg, the first European to print with movable types cast into moulds, could have walked into a newspaper office and instantly been at home. The quality of the paper might have changed. The speed of the printing presses might have been improved. But basically, the system had remained the same.

Today, things are beginning to move. Computer typesetting is making its debut, nervously with one eye over its shoulder. Satellite printing is becoming a reality. Instead of having to print and despatch from one point, newspapers can now transmit complete newspapers by satellite so that they can be instantly re-printed and despatched from regional centres throughout the country. And colour is beginning to appear in more and more newspapers.

Work is also under way on two further developments calculated to break the heart of any traditional newspaperman let alone Caxton or

Gutenberg. For, if adopted—and the chances are they will be adopted—they spell the end of the newspaper as we know it today. First, there is the television newspaper. Plug it in; turn it on; press the switch for instant newspaper and, instead of coming through the letter box, your newspaper comes straight out of the back of the television set. And if that is not enough, you can even have your own personal newspaper. Instead of taking a newspaper like everybody else you will shortly be able to dial your own newspaper, made up of the news you want; the stories you are interested in and, no doubt, the strip cartoons or photographs you don't like but look at if they are there.

It's enough to make Lord Northcliffe turn in his grave.

16 Customer Relations

'I said it in Hebrew—I said it in Dutch—
I said it in German and Greek;
But I wholly forgot (and it vexes me much)
That English is what you speak'

Hunting of the Snark

Ask yourself: Who's the most important person in any company? If you believe the managing director is the most important person in the company you're obviously going to go a long way. But, take it from me, you'll never be a salesman. For the most important person in any commercial organization in the world is the customer or consumer, the ultimate purchaser of the product or service. Without him, you're dead, no matter how sophisticated the accounting procedures or management techniques.

Yet all too often the consumer is the most neglected person in the world. Instead of seeing him as the foundation of the business, he is seen as a necessary irritant to be suffered in the cause of profit, like the businessman who wrote to the managing director of a large chain of hotels complaining about the condition of the bed clothes in his hotel room. By mistake, back came his original letter with the managing director's instruction to his secretary: 'Send this nut the bed-bug letter!'

Of all relationships a commercial organization has to develop and cultivate, nothing—but nothing—is more important than its relations with its customers. This applies whether you are selling industrial plant on a multi-million pound scale or washing-up liquid.

The starting point, therefore, is a company's reason for being in business.

Says Professor Theodore Levitt in his book *Innovation in Marketing*, '... the object of a company's efforts ought to be to offer a cluster of value satisfactions such that people will want to deal with it rather than its competitors'. The next point we have to consider, in that case, is what the customer wants. Professor Levitt gives an example, 'Thus if you sell pianos it is obviously critical to find out among other things what people buy pianos, who they buy them for and what all the problems are in connection with using a piano.' The answers he discovers are that '...

Adults buy pianos but mostly for their children. The piano is not just a noise making instrument or a pleasure giving tension-relaxing contrivance; perhaps for many buyers it is most important as a symbol of cultural elevation. They want their reluctant children to play an instrument whose presence in the house brings credit to the parents.'

But, of course, there are plenty of reasons why piano sales are nowhere near as high as the manufacturers would like. '. . . the resistance of children, the tediousness of learning to play, the competition of hi-fi and so forth. Hence to design a better piano, a more compact piano, a more beautiful piano, a cheaper piano, or to expand the number of retail outlets for them may be much less effective than developing a faster and more congenial way of enabling people to learn to play more easily', says the professor.

Given this reasoning, which is applicable to every product under the sun, we have the rational basis for a customer relations programme.

The product
The basic product, we assume, is acceptable to the consumer. If not, the whole selling operation is a fraud. I am not saying that every product must be so attractive and so valuable that consumers cannot resist buying it. That would be absurd. Instead, I believe, every product should have a basic consumer appeal otherwise sales would be minimal and the need for a customer relations programme non-existent.

Next, the product must be pitched at the right price. Like the politician, you can convince some of the people some of the time. But a successful product must be pitched at the correct market price otherwise, again, there is no sale and no customer relations operation. Finally, the product—and this is the first stage of any promotion programme—must be presented in the most attractive form for the consumer. The degree of presentation or packaging, of course, depends on what is being sold and varies from product to product. Try selling perfume in a plain brown envelope and you'll soon see why the packaging is so expensive.

Sales staff
This is the extension of the attractive receptionist syndrome. Basically there are two kinds of salesmen; salesmen who sell and salesmen who

handle enquiries from potential customers. Clearly, it is much better to have salesmen who actually go out of their way to sell. This might sound a truism. But go into any store any day of the week and you can spot the good salesman a mile away. It is in a company's interests, therefore, to select the right sales staff and train them to their own specific requirement.

New staff should be given a formal guide to any company, its philosophy, its products or services and its market. How often have customers been told by a member of a company, 'I don't know if they sell that; I'll have to check.' Apart from the obvious benefits of a more informed staff, it can help promote the sales attitude throughout the organization. Sales staff proper should be trained—not only in the use of the product they are selling but in salesmanship as well. This doesn't mean everybody should be a huckstering door-to-door salesman. It means that staff should be doing their job to the best of their ability. Think of the investment a company makes in a single salesman. It is foolish not to try to realize that investment.

Sales training is also a valuable safety factor, for it ensures that any sales force, by and large, follows the established selling methods. I say by and large because obviously nobody can monitor every sales opportunity encountered by every salesman. But it helps to cut down any extreme approaches.

Some companies go as far as writing out every possible sales approach and counter-approach imaginable. The sales force have to master these before they are allowed on the road. It might be mildly bureaucratic but it safeguards the company from extreme abuses and guarantees a fair response to the ultimate customer.

Sales promotion

This is the land of advertising and public relations. There are many definitions of different sales promotion activities. In the end, however, they are all aimed at presenting the product to the selected market in order to persuade people to purchase. The actual purchasing decision, however, has to be clinched by the salesman. Advertising delivers the customer to the doorstep. The salesman completes the sell.

Lesson number one is to present a consistent image to your market place. It is difficult enough trying to recall familiar names or signs. The company with a diffused image has little chance in establishing and maintaining any consumer loyalty. Having launched a consistent image, the next stage is to create the 'come hither' appeal for a product. This is either termed the 'value satisfactions' of the product if you're a follower of Professor Levitt, or the unique selling proposition, if you're a student of American marketing techniques. Either way, it means the sales promotion material must present the best possible argument for buying the product in the most attractive way. A good salesman does this automatically when he is talking to his customer. It is a little more difficult attempting the same thing on paper to a wide audience. It is largely because of this basic problem that so much advertising is accused of talking down to people. Unfortunately, it is a fact of life that those who complain, don't like plastic daffodils; those who don't complain do like plastic daffodils.

Overall sales promotion can stretch as far as sponsoring round-the-world yacht races or simply arranging taste-ins at local supermarkets.

Point of sale

Point of sale is virtually sales promotion on the shop counter. It is difficult enough, runs the theory, to get the potential purchaser inside the store. Then once inside, he is still faced with a bewildering choice. Point of sale material is supposed to swing him over that final hurdle.

The nearer we get to the actual purchasing decision the more careful must be the actual sales approach. The different provisions of the trade descriptions legislation control the sales information. The new credit legislation governs hire purchase terms and the true interest charges being made. Both are key figures in any customer relations programme. The more enlightened companies have anticipated these provisions in their sales promotion activities.

The sale

Now the sale proper. Everything so far as been designed to bring the consumer to the actual point of purchase. Now that we have brought him so far the problems are still not over. Not only the interests of fair trading but customer relations demand he is still protected from abuse.

First, the product must measure up in every way to the descriptions he has been given. Not only is this natural justice but it is also commercial commonsense since an angry customer is going to cause more time and trouble than the margin allows. An angry customer is also likely to damage the company's reputation as well.

Second, any accompanying guarantee must be spelt out in full. Schreiber Furniture Centres, for example, do this admirably.

Everybody buying furniture from any Schreiber Furniture Centre receives a written pledge from the chairman, Ch. S. Schreiber:

'I pledge the Schreiber Company to provide well-made furniture at fair prices; to honour delivery dates; and to refund or replace without delay if any piece of furniture is ever seen to be less than we claim.'

Which is, of course, the ultimate in customer relations. Whether other businesses follow suit or not this should certainly be their aim.

Third, any accompanying financial enquiries must be conducted with the consumer in mind. Most hire purchase or credit sales demand a credit enquiry on the purchaser. Because of the dangers of accusations about the invasion of privacy, the provision of inaccurate information and so on, it is becoming more and more prudent to inform the consumer that such a check is being made and to give them the opportunity to comment on any information provided.

Delivery

Mr Schreiber has already made the point about deliveries. Probably nothing causes so much ill will as delivery dates. Invariably, it is difficult to be quoted a delivery date; if a date is quoted it is rarely honoured. The customer continually complains. The salesman exhausts the goodwill he established in the course of the sale. By the time the delivery is actually made the credit supply is at an end.

Far better to follow Mr Schreiber's approach. Quote reasonable delivery dates—and keep to them. Nothing is more likely to win consumer goodwill. The situation is even worse in the industrial area. As a country we are recognized for our failure to keep delivery dates. As a result customers turn to overseas suppliers again and again. Not only is it in the consumer's interests that we solve this problem it's in the country's interests as well.

Installation

Once a product is delivered, the battle actually begins—especially if the product has to be plugged in and switched on or operated in even the simplest way. For I often believe this country leads the world in preparing instruction books that don't instruct, thus bungling up a major area of communication.

We've all experienced the situation. There is your brand new shining product. You've probably saved up for it. It is three weeks late on delivery. And there's the instruction book and you cannot understand a word. Or you get half-way through it and get stuck. There is a technical term you don't understand and so on. Nothing is more infuriating or likely to put you off a company for life. It seems so obvious. The first thing any company should do is make the customer appreciate its products. Yet nothing is so difficult. I've even come across British companies circulating instruction booklets in French and German to consumers buying their product in this country!

Putting out an instruction booklet that anybody can understand might not seem important in the total business context but it is invaluable in the eyes of the consumer.

After sales service

Stories about the poor quality of after sales service are legion. Communication again often breaks down on the part of the company. Many stories are also based on the after sales engineer turning to the broken-hearted consumer with the gallant enquiry, 'What did you buy this for then . . . ?' But the frightening thing is that they are probably right!

For some reason or other few companies believe in the value of a first-class after sales service. Which seems amazing. For, in my book, after sales service consolidates the first sale and prepares the way for the next.

We all know the fantastic success achieved by Volkswagen in their overseas sales territories. Within months of breaking in they seem to scoop up the sales. And the reason? They always consolidate their after sales service operation before they attempt to sell a single car. If a Volkswagen customer needs a spare part it's on the spot.

Many other manufacturers concentrate on sales from the beginning. As a result they are rarely able to keep pace with the speed and efficiency of the Volkswagen service.

Complaints

Straightaway, let me admit there are two kinds of people who complain: the professionals and the people who genuinely feel they have cause for a grievance. Unfortunately, however, both kinds can bring a company into disrepute. It is in a company's interests, therefore, as well as being natural justice to service any complaints as quickly as possible. A number of companies establish complaints departments to deal with customers. In some cases such a department operates under a fictitious name in an attempt to personalize the service and make the aggrieved customer feel he is dealing with a person rather than a machine.

Again, different companies prefer standard letters to deal with complaints while others operate a complaints questionnaire. Overall, there are only two rules when it comes to this critical area of customer relations: acknowledge all complaints promptly and act on all complaints promptly. Give every complainant the benefit of the doubt and you're unlikely to come unstuck. At the same time one should monitor the level and subject of all complaints. For the complaints department have often been able to show up the inadequacies of any quality control procedures not to mention any basic product deficiencies.

Customer as shareholder

The advent of consumerism coupled with the increasing democratization of share ownership has brought this area of consumer relations to the attention of more and more companies in recent years. And it works both ways. Companies are becoming more eager to turn investors into consumers and consumers into investors. For in the days of bids and counter-bids it increases company loyalty. New shareholders in consumer companies often receive a personal letter from the chairman as soon as their name appears on the register. Others include a booklet outlining the consumer products of the company concerned and the places they can be purchased. A few companies have gone a stage further and arranged factory tours and office visits for their shareholders. One brewery kills two birds with one stone by holding their annual general meeting at their head office which is then followed by a tour of the brewery. Some hotel groups have begun to consider cut-price shareholder weekends during the off-seasons of the year. Shareholders feel they are more involved with the company than simply filling in a proxy card at the time of each AGM. The company, of course, benefits by filling the hotels but, in the end, both sides are happy.

I have listed ten key areas for any company to examine their customer relations. The sooner they start the better.

Points for discussion

Comment on this statement: Of all relationships a commercial organization has to develop and cultivate, nothing, but nothing, is more important than its relations with its customers.

What do we mean by 'sales promotion'?

Why is the 'point of sale' so important?

What problems may arise when a product has to be installed after purchase?

What advice would you tender a company which sells 'consumer durables' as regards communications in its complaints department?

17 Press Announcements

'Contrariwise', continued Tweedledee, 'if it was so, it might be; and if it were so, it would be; but as it isn't, it ain't. That's logic.'

Alice Through the Looking Glass

Ask almost any businessman about public relations and he will say: press releases.

Next to the Chairman's Statement in a Report and Accounts nothing causes so much agony and exhaustion as the humble release. For basically, a press release is a press release is a press release. It's simply a straightforward way of informing the press about a particular event or occasion in the hope they will find it sufficiently newsworthy to pass on to their readers.

The problem, of course, arises when we begin to define 'News'.

We all know the old saying, Dog bites man is not news. Man bites dog is news.

But you tell me whether the appointment of a new chairman, the opening of a factory extension or the closure of a works canteen is news. The answer is, it all depends . . .

It all depends whether the chairman is 18 years old or 80; is a multi-millionaire or an undischarged bankrupt; or even a woman. It all depends whether the factory extension cost £2000 or £2 million; was designed by the works draughtsman or a duke; and is going to make dog biscuits or nerve gas. It all depends whether the works canteen is going to throw 1000 people out of work or one dozen; was infested with rats; or just served bad food.

And on that slim basis has been built a whole industry: the press relations business. But wait. Don't go away with the idea it's easy. It most definitely is not. For, it has been estimated, more than £1 million is regularly wasted every year by companies trying to get their names in the papers and falling flat on their faces. That works out at over 2000 tons of wasted paper and heaven knows how much time.

With so many people wasting so much time and money, the professional is obviously at a premium. And rightly so. For, I believe, companies not only have a duty to inform society about their activities,

155

society has a right to know what's going on.

As I have explained, daily business journalism made its debut on January 23rd 1884 with the publication of the *Financial News*. This was followed by the *Financial Times* on February 13th 1888. The financial press begat financial press relations.

Today the PR practitioner fulfils as much a key role in the corporate life of any company as a merchant banker or investment analyst. Or should do. For the growing trend towards consumerism and environmentalism coupled with the increasing hostility shown towards big business as a whole has forced companies into the public spotlight and, in many cases, forced them to explain their activities.

More than ever before, therefore, they need a public relations executive who can help them present their point of view.

Just listen to what the Confederation of British Industry has to say about the responsibilities of the British Public Company:

> 'A company should, as is indeed the practice of the best companies, pay proper regard to the environmental and social consequences of its business activities, and should not sacrifice the safety or efficiency of goods and services in the interests of expediency and competitiveness.
>
> 'In environmental matters, it is usually the company that is the first to know of a potential hazard or critical situation; it has a duty in such circumstances not only to take all possible remedial measures but also to inform the responsible authorities.'

As if that doesn't call for an active public relations programme, they go on to talk about 'points of contact with the public interest' and the steps companies should take:

> 'To be aware of the points at which the company does or may touch aspects of the public interest; to ensure that managers and specialists take account of this; to make due provision for this in forward objectives, policies, plans and financial budgets, and for performance to be monitored; by progress reports, internal and external, to show that the right balance is kept between short and longer-term objectives, between what is desirable and what can be afforded.'

If it wasn't before, the age of the consumer has now made press relations a vital management function for every company. Press relations ensures that shares reflect the financial and trading position as well as the future prospects of a company.

The City, we all know, recognizes merit. But it must be drawn to their attention. This does not mean chasing up the share price. Nor does it mean circulating wild rumours. What it does mean is running a straight-forward, informative press campaign to ensure the City has a constantly up-to-date picture of the company.

It is a fact of City life that information breeds confidence. Take two strictly comparable companies. It's a fair assumption to say that investors would tend to favour the one releasing a steady flow of information on its activities rather than the tight-lipped company. Inevitably that means a higher rating. One has only to look at the number of sleeping giants around to see the truth in what I'm saying.

Press relations is vital to shareholder education

It seems odd, to say the least, in a consumer-orientated world that the Government fusses over the consumer but virtually ignores the shareholder. Everything is being done to give the consumer information about goods in the shops; the correct weight, description, and so on. HP forms have to say this, that, and the other. Yet so long as the shareholder gets his annual report and accounts he should be happy.

A co-ordinated press relations programme fills in the gaps between one annual report and another. For surely it's in a company's interests to have a group of shareholders who understand the business and who can vote intelligently at company meetings. For shareholders, don't forget, can easily up and out. Shareholder loyalty can be invaluable in any bid situation.

Then there are prospective shareholders. If a company cannot attract prospective shareholders, it's virtually dead. An active market is good for the company. It is good for the shareholders.

Finally, institutional shareholders like Banks, Insurance Companies, Pension Funds, Trusts and so on. They are always looking for that valuable investment opportunity. An active press campaign will attract their attention.

Press relations is vital in assessing a business

Financial documents are usually out of date by the time they are published. Not least the annual report. An active press relations programme ensures a constant up-date on the state of the company and its activities.

The financial pages obviously feature the financial news. But there is also the remainder of the press to consider. The business pages generally are interested in company news. Special writers are also searching out new stories on different subjects. On top of that, there is the trade press. Years ago, probably the only newspaper with any following in the City was the *Sporting Life*. Today with the advent of analysts and research departments even the *Muckshifter* finds its way into different City offices.

Overall, the press can present both a wide-ranging and in-depth pictures of a company to a number of audiences.

Press comment is influential
Research studies on the City continually show that investors, banks and other institutions are for ever influenced by their research departments. But the research then goes on to show that research departments are influenced by the press more than any other outside factor. The press, and especially the key City press, is in the position of exerting more influence over the influence-makers than anything else. It follows, therefore, that any company wishing to influence the City should start with the City press.

The press, however, always dictates its own terms. It recognizes only its own authority. It cannot be made to genuflect to the board of any company let alone to a managing director.

Inevitably, this causes problems of status, response, respect and even security. In the end, however, both the press and industry can only benefit by a healthy, two-way relationship aimed at keeping the City informed on current developments.

Press relations divides the winners from the losers
In other words, those who communicate win, those who don't lose.

Examine the detailed cut-and-thrust of any recent takeover battle and you'll spot the same techniques employed by the winning side. For, more and more, takeover battles have ceased to be objective debates about the best position of a company. Instead, they have become almost highly-charged, emotional elections with the side responsible for generating the greatest loyalty carrying the day.

Details. Details. Details
The more details you release, the greater your chances of winning the battle. Details of the recent profit record. Details of an improving profit

trend. Details about expanding market shares. Details of new products.
Details of new management . . . and so on. The more details the better.

Technical data

The experts need their technical data to make up their own minds. The
mass of shareholders can just about tell the difference between a dividend and the divi! Yet the more technical data you give the experts, the
more they will come down in your favour and the more the shareholders
will follow their advice.

Go for the middle ground

Just as politicians go for the middle ground, so successful takeover companies should go for the middle ground which is made up of bank
managers, brokers and other influence groups. But never let them see
you're biased. Instead offer them objective summaries of your position;
objective summaries of shareholder reactions; and, of course, objective
summaries of press comment. They appreciate a man who doesn't ram
his ideas down their throat all the time.

Communicate direct with the shareholders

Just as everybody likes to read about their organization in the press,
they are even more flattered to be given the news before it appears in
the press. This is a way to any shareholder's heart. Let them see that
you honestly feel they are more important than the press by letting them
have copies of important company announcements before they are
published.

In the not-so-distant days, it used to be a case of those that mattered
knew and those who didn't know, didn't matter. But times have changed.
Not only do people matter but they must also be seen to matter.

Press relations enables a company to present its point of view

Or reply to its critics. And this is the dilemma at the heart of any public
relations function. For while public relations is supposed to explain
away any decision that creates a public outcry, it is rarely ever allowed
to contribute to the decision taking. You can hear a managing director
turning to the chairman, 'John's allright with the press but what does he
know about pricing policies or putting up factories in the Lake
District?'. Yet the managing director thinks nothing of getting his PR
man out of bed at one o'clock in the morning when he gets a call from
the *Daily Express* which has just been tipped off by a disgruntled
employee.

A professional PR practitioner will be able to represent his company at the bar of public opinion. He will be able to project his company's activities in the light of the growing trend to consumerism and environmentalism. He will also be able to explain his company's activities and plans. And, if necessary, he will be able to apologise if his company should inadvertently have failed in its duties in any way.

Having detailed the benefits of an active press relations programme, let me explain the way a company goes about getting itself in the news columns. As I have said before, there are no hard and fast laws about press relations. News is as unpredictable as the cocoa market. One day a particular approach works. Another day, it is as redundant as a bankrupt accountant. In general terms, therefore, there are three ways of implementing an active press relations programme; by personal contact; by press release; by press conference.

Personal contact

Obviously, this is the ideal approach. But it depends solely on the quality and the urgency of the news to be announced. Important stories demand the personal approach. Unimportant stories will wreck any personal contact on a continuing basis.

Press release

Basically, press releases are about the simplest art form imaginable: an objective announcement about a company activity or policy issued to the press in the necessary time with all the necessary facts. In practice, they are about the most difficult form of communication to achieve.

Take a press release recently issued by the Family Planning Association: 'How do people first learn about sex?' With it was a booklet containing, according to the press release, 'a wealth of useful facts and figures, some of which I hope you will consider worthy of reproduction.' With advice like that, who needs comedians? The trouble, however, is the lack of credibility the organization achieves among the press.

Press conferences

Press conferences can be anything from an informal meeting between a company chairman and selected City journalists to announce the annual figures to a full-scale presidential-style reception to fete the press.

The reason can be anything from a new appointment to a new product.

An aerial manufacturer once hired a public relations consultant to combat growing press criticism of the aerial lashings which were supposed to break loose in high winds. His solution was a press conference with a difference. He put an advertisement in the personal column of *The Times* for a female acrobat capable of doing vertical handstands from a great height. Immediately the story was taken up by the press who wanted the background. The result was a press conference on the roof of a tall block of flats in St. John's Wood where the lucky acrobat, a circus trapeze artist, proceeded to do a series of handstands on the horizontal bar of an aerial complete with standard lashings which had just been installed. The result: enormous press coverage and the end of any press criticism about the instability of the aerials.

Another manufacturer called a press conference to launch a new musical instrument, part-computer, part-organ selling at around £600. Because it was so easy to operate, they hired a chimpanzee to prove the point—and, of course, attract more publicity. The trouble was that after a few innocent chords, the chimpanzee promptly disgraced himself to the delight of the press if not exactly the manufacturers. 'Not only a performer but a critic too', said one journalist. Not all press conferences make such a big splash. Most are mundane. But properly approached and organized, they are an invaluable aid both for the companies concerned as well as the press.

Occasionally a company will go all out to exploit the press to its advantage. One of the best examples of this form of approach was the press campaign waged by Debenhams to fight off the take-over bid from United Drapery Stores in 1972. For ten weeks they up-staged UDS on one occasion after another and held the centre of the stage for themselves. The result was an impressive psychological victory that Debenhams were doing very well thank you, and anything to do with UDS would ruin everything.

Debenhams chairman, Sir Anthony Burney admitted that his strategy for success was simple. 'First, keep the initiative. Second, get your communications right with both shareholders and the financial press. Third, be prepared to defend in depth.'

From the moment Debenhams got wind of the bid the strategy was in full force.

Most aggressors issue their take-over bid late afternoon and then call a press conference to explain the reasons behind the move. Invariably they capture the headlines while the victim is thrown into utter confusion by the sudden offer and can only pull himself together long enough to say 'The bid is being considered by the board who will be announcing their decision shortly.'

Debenhams broke the rules and rejected the bid there and then. This was important as far as not only the press were concerned but staff and shareholders as well—and decisive, as it turned out. For it meant the defenders had scored a psychological victory in round one. Instead of reporting the bid and the usual victim's promise to consider it shortly, the newspapers found themselves reporting the outright rejection of a bid. The emphasis was on the reasons for the rejection—not for the bid. Both shareholder and staff morale was higher than ever. Everyone was immediately favouring the man with the courage to say No.

And, of course, the press knew Burney and Burney knew the press. 'I have always believed that a good relationship with City journalists is absolutely vital', he says.

Burney then decided to take the fight to shareholders and actively enlist their support. Posters and publicity material appeared in all 100 stores within the Debenham group. And in a move worthy of Barnum and Bailey, Burney despatched a record to every shareholder on which he had recorded his personal plea for them to unite behind Debenhams and vote against the bid. Which, of course, worked like a dream.

The publicity he was able to obtain for all these moves was enormous. The bandwagon effect began to come into operation. In the end, Burney only had to comment on this or that and it was immediately news. The attackers were in the shade and desperately trying to justify the reasons for the bid in the first place.

Burney not only knew how to handle the press, he had also mastered the intricacies of deadline and editions. On top of that, he knew when to keep his powder dry and when to use it. Faced with the counter-attack, UDS increased their offer. Burney shot it to pieces—but he kept back details of profit forecasts and property revaluations in case he subsequently had to fight off a second increase in the price. In the end it never came. But he had kept his ammunition in reserve just in case.

The Debenham's saga shows how a company can creatively use the press for their own purposes. It is worth bearing in mind when the telephones start ringing with more complaints about the environment.

Effectiveness

The basic question, of course, is always: How effective is press relations?

The answer depends on what you were hoping to achieve.

Some companies have been able to achieve enormous sales as a direct result of newspaper coverage. A manufacturer of a new-style plastic thatch notched up no less that £100,000 worth of orders as a direct result of the story in the *Sunday Times*. They also received an interested letter from ICI. Another company, specializing in electronics, landed a major export order from just one story on the Technical Page of the *Financial Times*.

Survey after survey has shown that when it comes to pulling in the enquiries, press coverage can often out-pull advertising by as much as seven to one. A leading manufacturer of floor cleaning and polishing machines analysed more than 25,000 enquiries they received from advertising, direct mail and press coverage in the course of one year in an effort to discover the cost per enquiry. In the end, they worked out that it cost them £5 to obtain one single enquiry through advertising; £1 by direct mail; and an economic 25p. by press coverage. They then went a stage further and worked out the number of enquiries which converted into sales. Direct mail rated 12 to 15 per cent. Advertising and PR tied at 20 per cent.

No doubt which was the most cost-effective approach.

Look at it another way. Each salesman probably costs around £12,000 to put on the road. Each call, therefore, works out around £8 a time—and how many effective calls does he make? Surely it is much better to use press publicity to land the enquiries and the sales force to follow them up.

And what was the benefit to Debenhams of their press campaign? Looked at in this light, press relations have a key role to play in the activities of any company and even more so in the age of the consumer.

Points for discussion

How do you define 'News'?

What is the CBI case for a company public relations programme?

Do you consider press relations as being vital to shareholder education?

Comment on the statement 'Press comment is influential'.

Are details important in winning a takeover battle?

What points, in your view, should be taken into account when drawing up Press Releases? (AIA).

18 A Communications Checklist

Now that we have looked closely at communication techniques, background and forms there are just a few questions you should ask yourself in regard to your company's communications policy. (I'm tempted to add the words 'if any' here, but am resisting the temptation!)

Has your company a policy for communications which is designed to ensure that its objectives and the general principles governing company actions are known and understood at all levels? Does your communications policy provide not just for keeping your employees informed of decisions that affect them directly but also for obtaining their views and ideas? Bearing in mind that management is the art of getting things done through people, you can't get things done unless you let your people know what your goals are, what you want to accomplish, why you want to accomplish it, how they will benefit from the result and the role they will play in accomplishing it.

Is there a formal communications system established in your works? If not, is the informal one that exists adequate? Are there properly organized regular meetings at each level of management? Is too much reliance being placed on oral transmission of all policy with too much room for distortion or are briefing notes issued by the senior management to assist foremen and office supervisors in interpreting and passing on policy decisions? Do you provide any training at all internally or by external attendance at courses or seminars for those of your staff who have to communicate with groups in their day-to-day functions? Is your internal communication system supplemented by a house journal, newsletter or other permanent record?

Have you a set policy for communicating information, where appropriate, to the mass media of the press, radio and television? Are appropriate PR agents working for you—either from within your own group or as outside consultants? Are you well reported generally? If not—why?

The following Ten Commandments of Good Communication seem a suitable note on which to end this manual on communication. They are reproduced by kind permission of The American Management Association Inc., in whom the copyright is vested.

Seek to clarify your ideas before communicating
The more systematically we analyse the problem or idea to be communicated, the clearer it becomes. This is the first step towards effective communication. Many communications fail because of inadequate planning. Good planning must consider the goals and attitudes of those who will receive the communication and those who will be affected by it.

Examine the true purpose of each communication
Before you communicate, ask yourself what you *really* want to accomplish with your message—obtain information, initiate action, change another person's attitude? Identify your most important goal and then adapt your language, tone, and total approach to serve that specific objective. Don't try to accomplish too much with each communication. The sharper the focus of your message the greater its chances of success.

Consider the total physical and human setting whenever you communicate
Meaning and intent are conveyed by more than words alone. Many other factors influence the overall impact of communication, and the manager must be sensitive to the total setting in which he communicates. Consider, for example, your sense of *timing*, i.e., the circumstances under which you make an announcement or render a decision; *the physical setting*—whether you communicate in private, for example, or otherwise; the *social climate* that pervades work relationships within the company or a department and sets the tone of its communications; *customs and past practice*—the degree to which your communication conforms to, or departs from, the expectations of your audience. Be constantly aware of the total setting in which you communicate. Like all living things, communication must be capable of adapting to its environment.

Consult with others, where appropriate, in planning communications
Frequently it is desirable or necessary to seek the participation of others in planning a communication or developing the facts on which to base it. Such consultation often helps to lend additional insight and objectivity to your message. Moreover, those who have helped you plan your communication will give it their active support.

Be mindful, while you communicate, of the overtones as well as the basic content of your message
Your tone of voice, your expression, your apparent receptiveness to the

responses of others—all have tremendous impact on those you wish to reach. Frequently overlooked, these subtleties of communication often affect a listener's reaction to a message even more than its basic content. Similarly, your choice of language—particularly your awareness of the fine shades of meaning and emotion in the words you use—predetermines in large part the reactions of your listeners.

Take the opportunity, when it arises, to convey something of help or value to the receiver
Consideration of the other person's interests and needs—the habit of trying to look at things from his point of view—will frequently point up opportunities to convey something of immediate benefit or long-range value to him. People on the job are most responsive to the manager whose messages take their own interests into account.

Follow up your communication
Our best efforts at communication may be wasted, and we may never know whether we have succeeded in expressing our true meaning and intent, if we do not follow up to see how well we have put our message across. This you can do by asking questions, by encouraging the receiver to express his reactions, by follow-up contacts, by subsequent review of performance. Make certain that every important communication has a 'feedback' so that complete understanding and appropriate action result.

Communicate for tomorrow as well as today
While communications may be aimed primarily at meeting the demands of an immediate situation, they must be planned with the past in mind if they are to maintain consistency in the receiver's view; but, most important of all, they must be consistent with long-range interests and goals. For example, it is not easy to communicate frankly on such matters as poor performance or the shortcomings of a loyal subordinate—but postponing disagreeable communications makes them more difficult in the long run and is actually unfair to your subordinates and your company.

Be sure your actions support your communications
In the final analysis, the most persuasive kind of communication is not what you say but what you do. When a man's action or attitudes contradict his words, we tend to discount what he has said. For every manager this means that good supervisory practice—such as clear

assignment of responsibility and authority, fair rewards for effort, and sound policy enforcement—serve to communicate more than all the gifts of oratory.

Last, but by no means least: Seek not only to be understood but to understand—be a good listener
When we start talking, we often cease to listen—in that larger sense of being attuned to the other person's unspoken reactions and attitudes. Even more serious is the fact that we are all guilty, at times, of inattentiveness when others are attempting to communicate to us. Listening is one of the most important and most difficult (as well being most neglected) skills in communication. It demands that we concentrate not only on the explicit meanings another person is expressing, but on the implicit meanings, unspoken words, and undertones that may be far more significant. Thus we must learn to listen with the inner ear if we are to know the inner man.

. . . even the Bible tells us, in the Book of Hebrews 'to do good and to communicate forget not'.

Bibliography

BLACK, Sam (1976). *Practical Public Relations*. London: Pitman Publishing Limited.

CARNEGIE, Dale (1957). *How to Develop Self-confidence and Influence People by Public Speaking*. London: World's Work.

CHAPPELL, R. T. & READ, W. L. (1974). *Business Communications*. London: Macdonald and Evans.

DEVERELL, C. S. (1974). *Communication*. London: Gee & Co.

GOWERS, Sir Ernest (1970). *The Complete Plain Words*. London: Penguin.

GUNNING, R. (1952). *The Technique of Clear Writing*. New York: McGraw-Hill.

LEYTON, A. C. (1968). *The Art of Communication*. London: Pitman Publishing Limited.

MEARS, A. G. (1966). *Speak in Public*. London: Elliot Right Way Books.

SMITH, C. Whitely etc. (1969). *Management Information: Its Computation and Communication*. London: Pan Books.

Index

168